The Art of Freedom

Freedom

A Guide to Awakening

T0127485

The Art of Freedom

A Guide to Awakening

Michael Damian, PhD

BOOKS

Winchester, UK
Washington, USA

First published by O-Books, 2017
O-Books is an imprint of John Hunt Publishing Ltd., Laurel House, Station Approach,
Alresford, Hants, SO24 9JH, UK
office1@jhpbooks.net
www.johnhuntpublishing.com

For distributor details and how to order please visit the 'Ordering' section on our website.

Text copyright: Michael Damian 2016

ISBN: 978 1 78535 593 6
978 1 78535 594 3 (ebook)
Library of Congress Control Number: 2016954850

A CIP catalogue record for this book is available from the British Library.

Design: Stuart Davies

Printed and bound by CPI Group (UK) Ltd, Croydon, CR0 4YY, UK

We operate a distinctive and ethical publishing philosophy in all
areas of our business, from our global network of authors to
production and worldwide distribution.

CONTENTS

Introduction

This book is about discovering freedom in the human experience. For freedom to be a practical possibility, it must belong to our reality. Freedom must mean that our real nature is benevolent and whole, and that our habitual sense of negativity and bondage is false no matter how convincing it seems. Therefore the search for freedom is best described as a search for reality.

We have always been told that to know the truth, we must awaken from the dream of mind. The dream is made of a primordial ignorance, or false mentality, that plagues the mind and adds immeasurable suffering to the normal challenges of life. Indeed, this ignorance blocks out the deep peace and happiness that would otherwise far outshine our challenges.

Those who love life, and who know they are one with all of life, also know that life is precious and meaningful beyond measure. Experiencing this truth for oneself depends first on hearing it. It's been said that although the truth is not in the dream, the truth can be heard in the dream. And the magic of life is that when you are ready for the truth you find it or it finds you.

We can recognize a teaching of truth because it resounds with simplicity, clarity, and heart. It does not lead you in circles. It does not seek to put you down or pump you up. It does not revolve around the teacher's personality. It simply affirms your deepest nature as consciousness.

The truth that we speak of is the timeless presence, the ineffable, intelligent awareness that has always been the fount of true spirituality, philosophy, and art. It takes some time to properly orient ourselves to truth, but it dwells always in the most simple and redeeming facts of our being. It is the sweetness and beauty of life as you know it. It is the healing touch of kindness as you know it. It is not something that can be reinvented or improved upon by extraordinary personalities. It is indestructible and pure, and it is you.

Therefore I speak to you of what you already know, yet which may not be entirely clear and stable in your experience. We are speaking of a life fully met and felt in consciousness, of the wonderful adventure life becomes when we clarify our nature and therefore our relationship to all things. We are speaking of the great and small uniting in an infinite value; the unity of love and wisdom revealed as your self.

To fully realize this truth you have to have the right spirit and attitude. You have to develop patience while you grow in faith, until that faith is transformed into effortless clarity. Take this process of self-inquiry seriously and it will soon lighten up your world. It will restore cosmic humor and direct knowing.

This book is offered to guide and inspire your process of discovery. Let your mind be spacious as you read. May you find the spirit of truth here, and may it reveal to you all that is good.

Michael Damian

1

Grace

At some time in our lives we sense that a great misunderstanding is at work within and around us. We sense that life is driven by a transcendent, ineffable intelligence that is somehow also our own deepest nature. We realize that our suffering is not caused primarily by events but rather by our own negative outlook and habits of mind. There also comes a budding recognition that we can transform this situation by examining ourselves and finding wisdom. Whatever wisdom may be, we sense its untapped potential within us. These intuitions mark the very beginning of spiritual awakening.

The process of awakening does not exclude any aspect of life, but it does frame all aspects in a greater context of truth. This is a living truth that has been perennially revealed and communicated across many cultures and ages. Sometimes called the perennial philosophy, this spiritual wisdom arises in our consciousness as the song of reality being sung through the human experience. Each human being reveals and sings this song in a unique way, but the song is universal.

Would you sing? If your experience were to shift from chronic emotional suffering to deep equanimity, from restless mental chatter to spacious clarity of mind, and from a lifelong sense of disempowerment and dissatisfaction to great ease and wholeness in your being—allowing you to navigate life's vicissitudes with full innocence and openness of heart—then would you sing?

Of course you would. And the notes would resonate in the hearts of others who sense the same music within them, who long to discover life as a conscious movement of creation and celebration instead of a constant struggle.

Since this opening of wisdom creates such a momentous shift

of identity and perspective in us, it has been described with dramatic metaphors like awakening or enlightenment. Indeed, this realization brings the sense of having woken up as if from a spell, or having come out of the solipsistic shadows of a confused mind and into a broad and effulgent light of pristine awareness.

Meanwhile, because enlightenment is still a fairly rare experience on earth, there are many myths about what this shift actually means and how it arises. Popular sayings and slogans point to it but often leave us more confused than ever. For example, it is often said that everyone is already enlightened. This is not exactly the truth, though it points in the right direction.

Our true nature is the ever-present light of consciousness. Enlightenment means to discover this reality. From the point of view of consciousness itself, there is no darkness and no enlightenment. There is no change at all in Reality. But from the point of view of a human being who does not recognize consciousness — even while being that very consciousness — experientially there is psychological darkness and a search for the unknown light.

On the experiential level, the fact is that unless and until we know our true nature with full clarity, we cannot consistently enjoy the happiness that is our birthright. We will wonder why we touch into deep states of joy and clarity only to find ourselves swiftly returned to the dreaded "real world."

The reason is this: Our habitual mentality is a confluence of reality and illusion that I call the *twilight state*. Twilight is caused by the blend of light and darkness. We are the light of consciousness in which all things appear but we cast shadows of thought and get lost in them. In other words, although everyone knows the immediate awareness of *I Am*, which is pure, intrinsically awake consciousness, we experience this light through the haze of mistaken identity and false notions. To know and experience our real nature we need only shine through this haze.

We dissolve the haze of twilight, egoic consciousness by using the light that we are. Use whatever light you have, and it will grow. I describe this contemplative process as a movement of *inquiry, insight,* and *awakening.* Spiritual inquiry, often called self-inquiry, begins when a deep question has arisen in our mind about the nature of self and reality, birth and death, suffering and happiness.

Inquiry is triggered by suffering. If it were simply our nature to suffer endless torment then no longing for happiness would arise. It is the intelligence and sensitivity of our real nature that gives rise to spiritual longing and inquiry in us.

We long for love because love is our nature. We long for oneness because oneness is the nature of reality. We are already experiencing oneness but we do not realize it. We do not need to expand ourselves into oneness somehow; we need only remove our confusion about the actual nature of things.

We have all pondered the meaning of life at times, but when inquiry becomes a focused, intentional search for truth and self-realization, then we can say that the search has begun in earnest. This begins a phase of intensive self-observation and contemplation. It generally induces us to take up meditative practices and study of spiritual teachings.

I call this a spiritual process because it centers on the ineffable, subjective domain of consciousness, which in old-fashioned language was called *spirit.* Whereas matter refers to visible, objective forms and movement, spirit means invisible, aware presence. To explore the spirit does not mean to reject or deny matter; it is only to ask about the nature of spirit and its relationship to matter.

The product of self-inquiry is fresh, direct insight into our identity. It is self-knowledge. In other fields of study we leave ourselves out. We gain knowledge about external things but this does not break the heart open or clarify the mind. Insight is a spark of illumination, born of the light that we are. Insight is the stuff of awakening, and awakening is the culmination of all insight.

Whenever we gain insight into our self-nature we shed a measure of falsehood. As we see through the false we start to experience our being more purely and sweetly than we ever imagined possible. When at last we have shed many layers of confusion our mind becomes predominantly silent, clear, balanced, and loving. Stripped of social artifice and defensive postures, the personality becomes refreshingly authentic and integrated. The mind rejoices in its own luminosity and expansiveness. This is called being near the goal.

The goal is reached in a moment when the primordial sense of doubt and distance created by our dualistic mentality fades away, and the undivided reality of consciousness knows itself. This moment cannot be understood or predicted beforehand, but it comes naturally as a result of your sincerity.

It is really that simple. If you have a sincere and abiding interest in truth then you will know the truth. If you are not very interested in truth then you have to suffer more, and life will make sure of that. Life will keep giving you rounds of experience and time to go through, until you sufficiently appreciate how you are exiling yourself from your own love and freedom by clinging to false beliefs.

Life on earth is a factory for making us conscious—that is all. It is very precise and elegant in this task. If life were not brutally efficient at delivering you the results of your false beliefs then it could not also deliver you the results of your receptivity, your yearning for real happiness, and your readiness to learn the truth about yourself.

Life gives you what you want, not what you think you want. Life in the general sense wants what is best for you, but life is also none other than your own being. And since you are free in consciousness, life must honor your freedom to choose for less than the best, for less than the truth. You do not have the choice to change the effects of truth and illusion once these effects are in motion, but you do have the initial choice between the two.

This primal choice exists in every moment. It is the point of grace and mercy in your life. The mercy is that no matter how wrongly you have chosen and how bad the effects have been, you have the freedom to choose again for truth, which means to awaken.

No matter how bad your dream has become, there is always an exit to the dream-state of mental chaos and false identity. When you choose rightly in a given moment you are effectively putting your attention back onto the real *I Am*, your sole place of empowerment and freedom. This ineffable, aware intelligence can never be objectified, located or defined in terms of something else. It is the root of the sense of self, beyond all self-images.

I Am is absolute, meaning it is not made of constituent parts. The world is full of things while you alone are not a thing. You are the pure knower of all things, states of mind and objective knowledge. That is why you can be in the world but not of it. You can wield objective, relative knowledge about the world without confusing yourself for one of the objects.

As you come to know your real nature, the superstructure of mental identity and imagination loses its support and gives way to light—the light of intelligent, aware spirit. The world of things remains but is now illumined and uplifted in your presence. The world becomes an intimate to you, so that you feel no real divide between your bodily form and other forms. On the level of form they are distinct and you honor that fact, but distinctions do not imply a fundamental separation. In fact, the distinctions only highlight the unified background of consciousness.

Naturally, this discovery often begins with extremes of wonder, exaltation, tears and laughter. It really is a cosmic joke you have been let in on, and that is why this laughter is like no other. It is the laughter of the universe that comes through you. When it comes you will be amazed to observe that it is truly *no one* who now laughs.

Of course, this cosmic somebody that you are is not literally nothing. It is pure consciousness experiencing its formlessness. In the world of things, seeing is believing. By contrast, the reality of consciousness cannot be seen or believed. It is only known and experienced directly.

You know now that you are conscious, but do you know that this consciousness is the sum and substance of reality? Until such non-dual understanding arises, all knowledge and spirituality is indirect and insufficient for the human heart, because you are not just this physical creation or social character. You cannot be satisfied by a pale reflection of your reality.

So make your choice. Moment to moment, choose again to seek the truth, to observe and contemplate this radical possibility. To actualize the happiness and love that arises from this recognition is the adventure of a lifetime. Your north star in this adventure is always your increasing experience of freedom, simplicity, and transparency of heart. This freedom and the happiness it reveals is the sole standard by which to weigh the fruits of awakening.

2

A Direct Path

Why is there so much confusion and struggle in the human experience? It is due to a core misunderstanding of the nature of reality, the only cure for which is understanding. This understanding is not a set of concepts but is an awakening and clarification of consciousness. It is self-realization. By realizing the true nature of self we come into accord with reality.

Most everyone understands that liberation of mind means becoming conscious in some way, but we generally do not understand the nature of the unconsciousness we are up against. If we did then it would no longer exist. The only way to begin dissolving our unconsciousness is to look very clearly and intently at it. This process brings our entire life into question, including everything we think, feel, and believe.

The effort involved in facing our ignorance is not measured in outward physical activity. It is an inward engagement of attention. Although awakening is often described as letting go of all effort and simply being, the practical fact is that checking the mind's habits of ignorance takes great attention and energy. It is the energy of interest, not force. The doing is in the listening and looking.

Although observing is a receptive process, it demands sustained intention and attention. All the spiritual platitudes in the world, no matter how comforting or inspiring, will not erase the specific aspects of unconsciousness an individual suffers from. In truth, everyone who finds freedom has done their inner work. They have looked at the true and false within themselves with greater and greater intelligence until they realized that pure intelligence as their own nature.

The way out of suffering is *through*. It is through yourself and all the particular blocks you have built up against love and truth, each of which contribute to the main block of mistaken identity.

You must take total responsibility for this process, for no one else can give you your freedom. Yet you are not truly alone in this. When you are fortunate enough to hear the truth and it resonates within you, then the truth will be with you from then on.

What is the truth? It is that you are not what you think you are. You are consciousness, divine intelligence. It is truth or reality because it does not change, vary or depend on anything else for its existence.

Though truth is beyond energy and all the games we play with energy, truth has energetic impact. It is a dynamic, transformative force that works to clarify and awaken our being from the inside out. By contrast, when you try to solve your energetic, emotional and mental problems at their own level, you only play with states of mind and at best create a brief sense of relief. Truth takes you beyond this frustrating approach to the direct experience of innocence and freedom within.

I can affirm that there are no short cuts, but you can take the direct path. The direct path is the most simple and sincere approach possible. It is based in a love for your reality, for that which has always been called the sacred, the divine. This love for the ineffable reality behind the appearance of life gives you the strength to face your pain without distracting yourself. Love gives you the strength to forbear, nothing else.

As insight grows you will learn that you cannot expect anything on this path except to realize freedom in your own experience. In this freedom there is pure love beyond the idea of what love should look or feel like. There is pure knowing beyond the desire to understand everything conceptually. And there is pure awareness beyond any effort to be aware.

Yet until you realize the effortless nature of consciousness, you will feel a sense of effort and desire—a desire to be conscious. The effort arises from your natural discomfort with suffering, and it will not abate until that suffering is dissolved. I won't tell you to drop your effort, because you cannot. I only tell you how truth works and how to understand what is happening. This helps convert the raw energy of effort and longing into clarity.

The sense of effort is the friction of intelligence working against the ignorance within you. It will fall away entirely when it has done its job. And then you will know beyond all doubt that you are free, that you are the living essence of reality, awake to itself while living an ordinary human life.

3

Intimacy

Fundamentally the mind can move in two directions—toward the false or toward truth. When the mind moves toward the false we narrow our perspective, harden our feelings and become fearful and confused. We may eventually get stuck in a web of deep delusion. When the mind moves toward truth we open in awareness, soften our feelings and gain peace. As we learn to observe and think along the lines of truth, the mind comes into accord with reality and the need to think dissolves into the simple clarity of pure awareness.

Mind is the gateway. Mind is all. Mind is consciousness, absolute reality. Freedom is found here in this ordinary mind or not at all. There is no getting rid of our mind, and there is no need to do so. We need only know its real nature. Mind is unlimited awareness, but we who are this limitless reality are entertaining an illusory confinement in mental creations.

If we go to war against the movement of thought then we have misunderstood the situation. The fact that we think and feel is not the problem. Nor is it a problem that we have a conditioned personality with unique strengths and weaknesses. The problem is only that, starting with false premises, our thoughts and emotions proceed on and on in the wrong direction until we realize we have to go back to the beginning and look at our premises.

The way to free the mind from the false is to observe it in light of a new perspective, which we call the teachings of truth. By truth we mean the non-dual wisdom that reveals totality. Who can say what is truth? Where does that authority come from? The answer only comes in your own experience of insight. When you understand, you do not *have* the answer—you become the answer. Ultimately, you are the only authority who can confirm wisdom or its absence.

In order to move toward wisdom there is no need for blind faith or belief. To make a beginning, we just listen to the wisdom teachings and develop provisional faith in their validity. This faith is a stirring of our own latent wisdom.

The teachings point out a new way to see. Without the reference point of the teachings we would be easily overwhelmed by the sheer force of our constant, confused conceptualization and the misery it creates. We would be distracted and lulled back into the dreams of the divided mind.

The first principle of the teachings is to take responsibility for the movement and quality of your attention. Attention means the focus or direction of observing. Initially, we cannot hope to stop all the negative, petty thoughts and feelings we find in our mind. They are the result of ingrained conditioning that cannot be dissolved all at once.

To find a modicum of power and leverage we have to go deeper than the conditioned level of mind. That place is what we already essentially are yet seldom appreciate — observing awareness. It is stable ground. The recognition that we can move attention off of thoughts and onto observing immediately introduces a greater sense of stillness — for the very atmosphere of the observer is stillness.

If there is one thing the conditioned mind feels threatened by, it is stillness. Stillness seems to be an abyss that threatens annihilation. Stillness is an ocean in which our false certainties cannot anchor. Whatever can sink will sink. This ocean is our own consciousness. Stillness is the way, but stillness does not mean holding still, holding tight. Stillness means letting be. It means observing. The inner sense of stillness arises naturally when our attention returns to the fact of observing.

By contrast, when our attention is stuck on what is always moving — thought, feeling, speech, body — then we identify with the moving stuff and feel ourselves in constant motion. What we call egoic consciousness is a kind of motion sickness. The cure, the way we get off the train of thought and emotion, is by observing.

Stillness does not mean that no thoughts happen when you observe. It just means that observing awareness is intrinsically steady, empty, and open. Sometimes we think that awareness comes and goes. In fact awareness never moves, only our attention does.

Although awareness is always here, this fact does not mean very much if our attention is regularly lost in the movement of thought and emotion. Until our attention is free from the pull of deluded thinking and rooted in effortless awake awareness, we are responsible for redirecting it.

Lack of attention, then, is the root of all suffering. Without attention we have no access to insight, and our growth is prodded slowly along by pain. We travel the default path of pain until we discover there is another possibility—the way of attention.

Lack of attention means a lack of intimacy with reality. Avoidance of reality plays out in our three most basic defenses: Denial, distraction and dissociation. We only fear reality because we do not know what it is. It can be terrifying to face the fact that we do not know who is doing all this thinking and feeling—who is living this life. So we deny the problem, distract ourselves and dissociate from our inner experience. We run from our own shadow instead of turning toward the light that makes shadows possible.

Sadly, entire lives are given over to the futile and destructive logic of escape, which only solidifies the bars of our imaginary prison. Our habits of avoidance never solve the basic problem of not understanding ourselves. Avoidance only warps our character and creates bigger and bigger crises in our lives.

In the absence of insight we become afraid even to look at the mess in our mind and to ask what is true. A mind terrorized by its own shadows is reluctant to pause and inquire. Its attention moves ever outward away from the silent, spacious core of self and reality, preferring to occupy itself with illusory comforts.

Despite our attempts at escape we continue to crave intimacy, contact and happiness of some kind. This craving in fact saves us. It forces us out of our isolation to encounter at least a bit of reality (other people) outside of ourselves. Insofar as we are drawn outward toward relationships and satisfactions in the world by our relentless urge to find happiness, the world confronts us again and again with ourselves.

We go out into the world partly to escape ourselves, perhaps by getting absorbed into another person, yet the world or the other person can only work as a mirror reflecting our inner state. This world of infinite experiences seems to contain great distances in which to escape and endless distractions in which to hide, but the world is really a place of intimacy. The world is our self and we cannot escape it.

To accept intimacy with self and world is the beginning of love. What you love you pay attention to, offering the energy of your focus and interest. Attention follows interest. When suffering finally grabs our attention we become interested in exploring its causes. By starting to pay attention we bring the most basic, rudimentary energy of love to a formerly loveless, neglected self or situation.

Love needs roots to grow, and the root is attention. This is why spiritual traditions so strongly emphasize the ability to be still, to observe the mind without running or strategizing for escape. Meditative observation is challenging to an unaccustomed mind. It reveals the stark difference between a frenetically driven, dazed existence and vivid wakefulness.

For example, imagine a security guard who spots a thief in action at midnight. The guard is physically wide awake but he becomes so fascinated with the scene that he starts to identify with the thief's goal. Without knowing it, the guard even begins to inwardly root for the thief to successfully pry the window open and make a clean getaway.

Would you say the guard is awake or asleep? Yes, the guard is observing the scene but he has become emotionally lost in what he is seeing. The real purpose of his standing watch has been hijacked by precisely that activity he was supposed to guard against.

Our relationship to the mind is just like this. We begin to watch the mind and then identification with mind quickly takes over. We are always aware to some degree, but just how awake is our awareness? Is it serving its true function? Are we able to discern between the causes of suffering and peace?

To know what we are up against, we can acknowledge that there are degrees of unconsciousness. There is a kind of suffering in which we are numb even to the fact that we suffer. For example, someone who is often angry might not realize that anger is a form of suffering. They are identified with it and find it morbidly comforting. It affirms their identity and sense of power. Eventually, this pattern will catalyze an event that will create enough pain to inform the person that chronic anger is a deep form of suffering.

Suffering is not senseless. It has an intelligence that lets us know something is off. When our suffering finally convinces us to observe and question our mind in a consistent and purposeful way, then we have begun the work of liberation. We have taken responsibility for our mind and our experience.

Depending on how we use it, the mind can obscure or reveal truth and thereby create hell or heaven for us. In that sense, where we really live is in the quality of our state of mind. The factor that determines its quality is insight.

Insight comes from attention. Insight clarifies and uplifts.

Insight also changes us at the deepest level of identity, because to see things as they are creates a shift in who we think we are.

In other words, by seeking the truth, we awaken in truth. We cannot say, "I want to know the truth about existence, but leave me out of it." It does not work that way. To ask about the truth of existence throws our own identity into question. It works this way because truth, being total, cannot be found as an object, image or opinion outside of you. It is known through direct identity or not at all.

Insight is the inner vision that penetrates the surface appearances of life, freeing us from the toil of illusions. Vision has to start somewhere. We begin by seeing what is in front of us, whatever is appearing in the mind. As we learn to see, the passion for seeing grows. Vision opens the horizon of beauty in the heart. Then the time comes when we receive the total vision of the divinity of all things, in which the self is opened forever.

Opened, we enter true relationship. This is why enlightenment has been described as intimacy with all things. Intimacy implies the closeness of knowing. This does not mean that enlightenment will fill us up with knowledge about everything. Intimacy refers to a different order of knowing, through love. Love is a condition of vivid comprehension in which we appreciate that reality is whole and benevolent. This comprehension is the supreme discovery, the unknown goal toward which all human desire is bent.

Love is the power that reveals truth and drives our search for it. You may have noticed that if you study something deeply—an animal, a face, a piece of music—you begin to love it. You become one with it. This felt sense of oneness is the highest expression of love. When you love like this you transcend the selfish distortions and ambitions that once tainted your study. A true study and mastery of anything both demands and evokes this real love.

In the study of existence you realize your oneness with it. As the artificial divide between you and the world dissolves, the whole of existence is found to be good and worthy of love. All sense of separation is gone. There is an open, lucid awareness that manifests the joy of being. When we are joyful we do not think to go and find God. In joy we feel light as a feather, and in that lightness we know God and all that is worth knowing.

The spiritual search is for this undivided condition. In this search, as in all things, you need understanding and you need love. The way is to lovingly work with your present understanding, knowing that love directs the work and already contains the goal.

It is love that drives you to seek understanding, and each new step in understanding brings more love. When you lack understanding in any given moment, you are saved by your love, even if that love cries out in despair. Love ensures that revelation will eventually come like lightning, and love itself will be the light in it. So welcome the wind, the storm and the rain as you inquire into your true nature. They bring the lightning of self-knowledge. And in a flash you will behold a new heaven and earth, and know yourself as you have always been.

4

Liberation

It's time to break the alarm clock
that's been ringing all morning and wake.
It's time to shake the haze of thought
off your head and stake your life
on the brilliant stones of this morning.

It's time to hear the one voice in your dream
that isn't sighing, crying or intellectualizing.
It's time to part ways with the lonely fiend
and walk in the golden hills of soul company.

It's time for you, it's time for me to be
outrageously at ease amid complexity's
absurd pretense.
It's time to watch the grandiose
stage of suffering collapse into the heart's
unthinkable lightness.

My teacher threw an alarm clock
into my dream, not to ring in
another day of sleepwalking
but to announce love's homecoming theme,
a funny show of tossing and turning
that ends in the simplicity
of rising.

As a child I had the feeling that I would be happy in old age. I felt
connected with something timeless and wise. It was a quality I
could not yet fully access but which called me forward to its

wholeness.

Back then I did not know that this quality was an aspect of our spiritual nature. My mind projected that quality forward in time as the image of a wise and contented old man. There was some truth in that projection though, because it generally does take some time and experience to get to the essence of things.

Fortunately, I did not have to wait until old age for that timeless presence to come to the forefront. At the age of 31 I died to my self and my world as I had imagined them. I woke up out of imagination to the ineffable reality that is both the essence of who I had always been and the transcendence of every self-image I had ever entertained. I realized pure consciousness as my nature and the ground of existence.

That recognition released and redeemed every moment I had ever suffered through. All the shadows of happiness I had ever chased were illumined by their fathomless source, the pure joy of being.

I had tasted that joy many times before in smaller doses. These were moments when I felt fulfilled, stable and inspired by life's possibilities. Yet such moments inevitably gave way again to ennui or dissatisfaction of some kind. The source of dissatisfaction was always a basically fearful and negative assessment of myself, others or life.

I want to describe how that condition came to an end in my case. The first point is that I searched for truth because of two contrasting experiences: suffering and happiness. When I suffered I wanted to stop suffering. And when I was happy I wanted to remain happy.

I began to focus on the question of happiness toward the end of my university years. I was spending a semester in Amsterdam where my grandfather was born, when this immense question came alive in my mind. There I was tantalized by my first glimpses of deep awareness and lucidity. As I explored the world and studied its history and politics, I felt a sense of timelessness within time. I felt the preciousness of my life as a chance to come to full consciousness, to understand and to be free, whatever that might mean.

I keenly felt the world in myself and my self in the world—the personal and the universal inextricably enmeshed together. It was as if life were opening itself to me saying, *"Know me. Find the golden thread that's woven through all time and space. It lies within."* But when I pulled on that thread it led straight to the knot of angst at my core. I knew I had to deal with that knot.

At the end of that semester I made a solo journey to the Alps. Exiting the train I entered a snow-covered landscape surrounded by mountains. With headphones tucked under my wool hat, I would listen to a cassette tape of Bach as I hiked for hours in pristine wilderness. This was perhaps my first archetypal experience of solitude, and I was filled with exultation as I suddenly received and knew that happiness in this life was completely up to me. But how could I live up to such a demanding truth?

I returned to Amsterdam for a few final days. My roommate Paul was already gone and had left a farewell letter on my desk, as we did not have cell phones at that time. He ended his thoughtful letter with these words:

The world is bright. The mind is dark.
But the only men who make their mark
are those who fight the persistent haze
and help the others through the maze.

Here was the Buddhists' bodhisattva vow, the Judeo-Christian call to serve others, and the struggle of consciousness to rise out of humanity's ancient confusion. Paul's words summarized the revolution in perspective I was going through. I was beginning to see the inner life of the mind and spirit as primary. The stage was set for me to eventually give up on world affairs and become a psychologist.

After graduation, life presented me with some practical questions: What shall I do with my life? How can I help? What will fulfill me? For the next few years I wrestled mightily with these questions. They brought me to confront my assumptions about who I was.

We are conditioned to build our self-image along familiar lines and to continue in a known direction. Meanwhile the greater intelligence of our being works behind the scenes to create new openings, uncertainties and serendipitous events that loosen the mind's grip and hint at a fresh direction.

Friends would urge me to go ahead and get a law degree or become a professor of English. At one point I was ready to move to the South Pacific and become an anthropologist. Searching for the origin or essence of humanity, I was fascinated by prehistoric journeys across the ocean and places untouched by modern civilization. If I went on such journeys and visited such places, perhaps I could reconnect with something primal, pure and free that we had all apparently lost.

My dissatisfaction gnawed at me like a starving but faithful dog, and prevented me from accepting easy answers. This struggle over the question of purpose pushed me to explore philosophy and psychology in search of answers. It ultimately forced me to rediscover the contemplative, spiritual temperament and affinity for Eastern philosophy that I knew in childhood. I had become too narrowly identified with the intellect that got me through college. When I realized that my deepest interest was to understand the nature of mind, meaning, self-actualization and happiness, the way opened for me and the answers came.

One of the most succinct Zen teachings, from Dogen Zenji, states that, "To study the way is to study the self. To study the self is to forget the self. To forget the self is to be enlightened by all things." As I look back at the perfection and grace of this process, it is clear to me that enlightenment is not an entirely discontinuous, sudden break from life as we know it. A momentous breakthrough of illumination is only the most noticeable manifestation of grace. The mostly hidden movement of grace lies in its quiet, continuous action in our everyday lives.

The world of enlightenment interpenetrates us all along. Our true nature is already present, albeit in a latent, unknown state. We realize and actualize it from the inside out. The paradox is that the fullness of time serves to reveal the timeless—the eternal presence which is the divine subject of all our personal and collective histories.

The conditional, external world of circumstances and the unconditioned, conscious order of being are not in conflict with each other. They are in absolute harmony because they are one.

This is why I honor my past struggles and I urge you to honor your struggles, past or present. We can honor our struggles insofar as we understand the purpose they serve. As solid and soul-crushing as the contingent, time-space world sometimes seems to be, it will turn to light at your request. The problem is that you may be asking for the wrong things, when the only thing you can or should ask for is consciousness.

Our first and final freedom is to become conscious. Free will does not mean you can choose to alter what reality is. It means you are free to wake up to reality. Yes, we are always free to choose among illusions—and many people spend their lives doing just that—but our real freedom and power is to finally choose full consciousness. Perhaps we are afraid to make such a consequential choice. The truth awaits in stillness while we tremble at its immensity and power. Happiness, we easily fancy that. And love is eminently alluring. But when we sense their gateway is to become fully, irrevocably conscious and responsible beings, we falter. We are not sure we could stand being that powerful, alive and free.

At first, consciousness feels like a burden, but it is the right burden. By bearing it you become lighter. It enlightens you and you wonder why you ever feared your own freedom. All of our suffering is about carrying the wrong burdens until we consent to carry what is truly ours to carry, which is consciousness. You carry that weight until it turns to light, until you are that simple and pure light of being.

Until we drop it, it is hard to appreciate how heavy the burden of unconsciousness is. Since it takes the shape of our own mind and body, we equate its heaviness with reality itself. We think, *This is just how life is.* How can we fathom what our mind would feel like without its ancient fear and separation?

There was a Zen teacher who spent time in a mental hospital after his great satori. When a student asked him why that was necessary, the teacher said it was due to the great burden he had been carrying, which was let go all at once. Letting it all down in a flash of illumination was a tremendous shock to his system. Freedom is a dizzying thing at first, and it is normal to go through a period of disorientation after awakening.

The story of how I let down my burden continues with my search for a vocation in my twenties. At one point I worked with a life coach and I enjoyed the process. Sometime later, I got the idea that becoming a life coach would allow me to earn a living while I figured out my calling. I immediately signed up for a weekend training.

As soon as I walked into the hotel's conference room I was plunged into an exhilarating world of self-discovery. Everyone was there to create a more fulfilling life and to learn how to help others do the same. The weekend was an epiphany for me. To my great joy I realized with total certainty that my role was to facilitate personal growth and well-being.

The workshop triggered breakthroughs for many of us. We were guided to confront limiting beliefs, let go of self-image concerns and take the risk of authenticity. Many of the exercises had a Zen-like quality, demanding that you speak or act spontaneously, without suppression or rationalization. I got to practice working one-on-one with people and felt completely at home in that mode. I would surely become a coach.

By the end of the second weekend training, however, I was disturbed. This was a culture that emphasized personal empowerment through the passionate pursuit of your desires. By naming your desires you were supposed to identify your core values and aim to live them. A coach's task was to help you clarify your values and hold you accountable.

I questioned this formula. Most of the desires people voiced were material and external. Everyone was trying to figure out exactly which external arrangements and accomplishments would lead to happiness. For me there was not enough emphasis on the need for self-knowledge and wisdom in this equation.

I was gradually drawn away from coaching and toward a deeper study of psyche and spirit. I was taking a few psychology classes at a local university, when a classmate suggested that my existential sensibility would be put to good use as a psychologist, and then I could also do whatever kind of coaching I wanted.

Around that time my reading turned from literature and poetry to depth psychology and spirituality. I read Carl Jung, M. Scott Peck, Shunryu Suzuki-roshi, and a few Buddhist psychologists. These diverse voices spoke of a world in shambles, a humanity enslaved by trauma and suffering, and yet a perfection of Being that shined through it all.

When I read *Memories, Dreams, Reflections* by Carl Jung, I knew that I must become a psychologist. Instead of helping people fulfill their personal dreams, I became intent on understanding the structure of the collective egoic dream and the cure for our many nightmares, which is to awaken. When I discovered there were graduate programs where I could study clinical psychology and spirituality together, my path was clear.

In 2002 I moved to California to earn my PhD in clinical psychology. At my graduate school there were no grades given, and there were hardly any chairs in the classrooms at that time. We all sat on cushions, as if to begin the inner journey where we would inevitably end up—on our butts, humbled, crawling for the nearest box of tissues. The root of the word humility means earth or ground.

While studying theory, our cohort also plunged into individual therapy, groupwork, creative arts, somatic work, and countless impromptu counseling sessions performed on each other. In the first few years I came face to face with all of my heartbreak, fragmentation and defenses. I underwent many emotional catharses and shed layers of persona. My demeanor changed. After one powerful catharsis even the tenor of my voice became softer. As I opened up to my pain I also felt others' pain more deeply. For example, I could no longer watch violent films without wincing inside.

I also healed my body of chronic pain, practiced yoga and took dance lessons. During these years I was an amateur percussionist playing Latin and Afro-Brazilian music. I enjoyed performing, dancing and socializing in the music scene. The life of rhythm and motion opened up a great sense of vitality and enriched my life for many years. However, I was rather dependent on music for the sense of connection and aliveness.

As I finally internalized that vitality, my attachment to music fell away. Playing and listening to music went from something I could not live without to something that could no longer fulfill me. I increasingly longed for something beyond any sensory pleasure or positive self-image. I began to rest in silence more often. I wanted to be free.

Toward the end of graduate school my focus on spirituality intensified. I began to feel there was something entirely too indirect and incomplete about most psychological approaches of healing, as if a great truth were thundering off in the distance but at such a low frequency that few could hear it. In time, that thundering was all I could hear.

Even at our holistic graduate school, spirituality was usually seen through a watered down, relativistic perspective as whatever makes you feel more centered or connected. I noticed that we all seemed to be searching endlessly in the mind and body for the explanations, healings or intuitions that would bring freedom. I saw that it did not matter whether you were a so-called heart type or head type, whether you focused on traditional psychology or new-age beliefs and practices; the fact was that if you identified with your concepts, feelings and self-construct, then you were living in your head. Your pursuit of healing took place within a self-created bubble of imagination—of subjective beliefs and feelings considered sacrosanct despite their ephemeral nature. The healing could only go so far and then no more.

Did anyone else notice the gaping abyss of silence inside, just behind all the shifting moods and states of mind? This abyss was where I was headed.

At the age of 31, after several years of training as a psychologist and more than a year of personal Jungian therapy, I felt more stable and self-actualized than ever. I began to trust my instincts and insights.

One of the themes of my process was to reconcile the masculine and feminine aspects of mind. Like many men in our field, I sought to access the feminine qualities, but sometimes this created an unnatural imbalance. I found that as I integrated the more receptive, feminine values I no longer needed or wanted to display the phony, compulsive sensitivity found in many spiritual men.

As I accessed the feminine values in my own being, it made me less needy toward women and less moody. Instead of making me less masculine the process landed me in a more conscious masculinity. Instead of trying hard to connect and to prove that I care, I learned to express empathy while maintaining appropriate boundaries. I let go of wanting to save people and I was no longer drawn into dramas.

I saw that the egoic mind of a spiritual seeker tends to mimic spiritual qualities. It is engaged in a compulsive show of virtue, an attempt to always appear sweet and loving. This spiritual façade has nothing to do with real love or consciousness, and I was thoroughly sick of it in myself and in others.

Once I reached this point of disillusionment with mind and world, I keenly felt the need to go further. I still suffered moments of self-doubt and constriction, and would wonder if there was still something broken or unhealed within me. The mind always amplified such worries while overlooking the fresh potential of the present moment. Its strategy for healing was always to seek out more concepts and processes.

I sensed that the struggle and search for wholeness could go on forever. I could believe in the paradigm of an always broken self in need of this vague thing called healing, and I could wear my struggle like a badge of authenticity, or I could investigate what lies beyond the conditioned mind.

For some time, my faith toggled between the psychological, relativistic approach and the teachings of absolute truth. Yet my attention was drawn again and again to the message of freedom I found in spiritual teachings. Eventually, I was convinced that the only real solution to suffering was enlightenment, a total shift of view and identity.

And so there came a time when I stopped trying to fix myself with tricks and techniques. I stopped attending conferences and workshops that promised more empowerment. I embraced my inclination toward solitude and contemplation, taking silence as my main teacher. I only wanted to be in the company of truth.

And then the moments began to come when truth would

announce itself in a beatific sense of glory, clarity and rightness that could never have been predicted. Contact with the sacred, both in dreams and in waking life, brought new vision and faith.

So this beatitude was the cure—not sifting through emotions and explanations. Carl Jung described the healing power of the sacred when he stated:

> *The main interest of my work is not concerned with the treatment of neuroses but rather with the approach to the numinous. The fact [is] that the approach to the numinous is the real therapy, and inasmuch as you attain to the numinous experience you are released from the curse of pathology. Even the very disease takes on a numinous character.*

We cannot neglect the process of becoming familiar with our neurotic patterns and pain, but in order to be transformative, this process must be situated in a greater, transcendent context or experience. According to Jung, that context was found in consciousness, through an ethic of personal spirituality beyond religious dogma and cultural conformity.

Jung's view was that to know God, one has to become a conscious individual; and to become a conscious individual, one has to open to the mystery of God. We encounter that mystery in the soil of our personal struggles and contradictions from which we alone can harvest meaning—and from which no outside authority can save us. Unless the bounded personality, with its range of primitive and sophisticated defenses, could be opened to the destabilizing experience of the transcendent sacred, the search for healing would always be hijacked by the collective trance of ego.

Jung also spoke about the meeting of two personalities as a chemical reaction and a healing factor. I encountered many resonant souls on my way. One of them was a wise friend, a few years older than me, whom I had met a few years before graduate school.

In the spring of 2003 I returned to New England to visit family. I also drove to the Berkshires to see this dear friend and have the usual long talks over tea. At the end of my visit she handed me a set of cassette tapes to borrow. It was the audiobook of *The Power of Now*, by a relatively unknown author named Eckhart Tolle.

I listened to the first tape as I wound my way through the country roads of Connecticut. And as I listened, I was changed. Eckhart cataloged the worldwide symptoms of human insanity and pinpointed its cause: our unquestioned, slavish identification with the mind. Within a few hours he summed up my deepest convictions about the human condition and how we can transform it through awareness.

This pure teaching went into me like rain. It radically simplified my mind and quickly began to dissolve my remaining self-construct. I knew that his teaching held far greater wisdom and healing power than what most of psychology or popular spirituality offered.

My recognition of observing awareness created an immediate energetic shift toward greater peace. During the next few years I worked to bring conscious presence to every moment. It is true that conscious presence, like the present moment, never goes anywhere, but our attention does. It gets lost in the habits of attachment and identification.

This initial sense of making an effort to awaken is unavoidable. It is due to the constant need to withdraw attention and allegiance from the habits of illusion. It takes no effort to be what we already are—the effort is only to establish vigilance and remembrance of it.

From then on I never let the truth out of my sight for long. I focused on meeting everything and everyone with the stillness of presence instead of mental noise, as one of my favorite Eckhart pointers advised. Once we have recognized presence, it naturally exerts a will to remember itself. We experience that will as a personal choice and desire although it is actually a spontaneous movement from our true nature.

In the spring of 2006, the desire to live a fully liberated life became urgent and overwhelming. Despite my contact with the peace of awareness, I still identified with the mind. I did not understand the infinite nature of consciousness, oneness or reality, and this became unbearable to me.

By then I was thoroughly disillusioned with the attempt to gain self-worth in any identity or achievement. Feeling the need to put truth first in my life, I dropped all effort to maintain social activities that distracted me from my purpose.

As my attention turned inward I spent more time in solitude and study, often walking and meditating in nature. I had a few powerful peak experiences. More importantly, there came the foretaste of a deep and simple freedom. On one summer evening I wrote these words down:

Rainy night.
I pray for nothing more
than to see an old iron bell
swinging like a drunkard
with ecstatic emptiness.

Wind blows through me too
and I'm more thankful for things.
I'm happy I've danced and I'm happy
I've sat in the corner thinking.

Everything had to be suffered
before everything
could be empty again.

Everything makes me cry

as though I were
returning home.

It occurred to me that I should find a teacher who could offer feedback and guidance. I had heard of a local teacher named Adyashanti and decided it was time to attend a talk and listen to his tapes. I found that his energy matched my sense of urgency and conviction. While Eckhart's first book set out the overall view with great simplicity, Adyashanti's talks addressed more of the nuances of the journey.

Adyashanti suggested that awakening was best approached with a blend of heartfelt receptivity and focused inquiry. For example, on the first side of one of his cassette tapes, he spoke about the willingness to be fully touched by life. To feel deeply and shed tears of grief was different than to suffer. In fact, much of our suffering lies in the fear and refusal to feel.

To regain our childlike openness of heart means to risk falling apart and appearing to be a fool. If you want to be free, he said, that is a risk you have to take. You have to be free to be a fool in the eyes of others.

On the other side of the tape, Adyashanti spoke forcefully about our true identity. He declared that each of us is already the buddha—not as a metaphor or a nice idea to have, but as an absolute fact whether we knew it or not. He continued: *"We realize we are the buddha, simply, when we stop telling ourselves that we are not."*

The significance of this statement hit me in waves. Whereas the first phase of my inquiry had focused on calmly watching and accepting thoughts and feelings, this phase was focused on using the blade of discernment to cut away every last tether to the false identity.

With the understanding that moods, emotions and thoughts do not define my true nature, I had resolved that I would stop granting them the power of my belief and identification. I would break their energetic grip on my being—not by suppression but by constantly seeing my true nature as awareness. And that is exactly what happened.

On the day I heard Adyashanti say, *"You are the buddha,"* the waves of understanding silently knocked out my identity as a spiritual seeker, and even as a person. This was a dawning of pristine awareness beyond all divisions and parts. Instead of feeling awareness as a spacious quality of the mind or person, I awoke as pure space, pure knowing.

In the quiet dawn of realization there was a great sense of death and completion, as though an entire life had ended and all its contents were fully loved and redeemed. All was fresh and timeless as though I had entered the uncreated eye at the center of creation.

A deep stillness unfolded. In that stillness was the awe and wonder of an absolute aloneness beyond every created thing, yet without any loss of ordinary perception. Nothing outward had changed, but the sense of being a known mental or physical object had collapsed, taking down with it the diaphanous boundaries of the dream-self.

Life was immediate, unmediated, charged with presence. An unworldly silence prevailed, along with the most delicate and immense sense of love I had ever known—a love without object. I was drenched in the original innocence of being, and I was the innocence.

A few days after that shift, I joined some friends at a restaurant by the ocean, where my friend would be singing jazz songs for the evening dinner audience. When we sat down for dinner I noticed that I was intoxicated with bliss. I was helplessly, wordlessly gazing at people.

One of our companions noticed my strange state, so I explained that I was having some spiritual experiences. She casually replied, *"Oh I see. So you're pretty Zen right now."* As soon as she said this a wild laughter erupted from me and rolled on uncontrollably.

When the laughter finally settled, some tears started to well up yet without any emotion, and my body was seized with rapid breathing. In the next instant there was a rush of radiant energy like a lightning bolt from the ground up out the top of my head — and then there was only absence.

I do not know how to explain that absence except to say it is an absence from which so much never returns. It is like sailing over a horizon where concepts permanently lose their grip on the world.

When awareness of the world returned, I was sitting in perfect, supreme peace at the table, eyes closed. Some soft laughter rolled out from that emptiness. It was the laughter of the universe, beyond all sense of personhood. There never was anybody separate from pure consciousness, pure existence. The dream of separation was absolved in the absolute. Self, reality, was nothing that could be captured by thought, image or perception.

That evening by the Pacific Ocean, I was as if reborn. If you have ever prayed to be cleansed, this was the ultimate cleansing by the rain of infinite reality. Traditional yogis want to stop the waves of the mind in order to get to nirvana. But you do not exactly get to nirvana. Nirvana gets you, and then you as you knew yourself are gone. It may sound nihilistic but the reality is anything but empty or meaningless. It is the meaning and fulfillment of life. To seek and ask for this truth-consciousness is no game of self-improvement or escape from life. It is to ask for the lightning of utmost life.

Following this shift I experienced life from an inconceivably different vantage point. For me to describe this new experience to friends and family was like telling them that I was from Mars.

For many days I experienced an extreme silence of mind in which very few thoughts arose. The energy of thought was so neutralized that it took a great effort to speak. To speak felt like a chore, a trivial task to be performed up there at the surface of mind.

This silence was a holy and intense experience. Even more poignant than the silence was its cause—the knowledge of being nothing other than this cosmic, absolute reality. The silence was a symptom of release, known as *moksha* in Sanskrit, from the ancient illusion of the mind and world.

Imagine, for example, how sweet the sunlight would feel to a prisoner who has just been freed after spending many years in a dark prison. As good as the light would feel, the sense of freedom would be the greater joy behind it, and the source of all the sweetness to come.

The idea that this freedom might disappear never entered my mind. There was the awareness of a permanent shift, because what awoke to itself was timeless consciousness. At times, people describe awakening as a powerful experience of transcendence that comes and then goes. Some teachers warn that such awakening can become a memory that the mind uses as a reference point. They emphasize that we must keep awakening in every moment.

I can only say that such words do not apply to genuine awakening or, to use a more precise term, realization. If you truly realize that your nature is consciousness, it cannot exactly be called a "moment" of awakening, for that emphasizes temporality and partiality. By definition, if it is merely a moment or a memory for you, then it was never realization of timeless truth.

When I refer to realization, I am not speaking of glimpses of oneness or seeing that the self-image cannot define you. I am speaking of the irrevocable seeing of true nature, absolute reality, which has been called a turning-about in the deepest seat of consciousness, entering the stream, or gnosis.

There are well-known ways of ascertaining genuine realization from partial insights and subtle mind states. The signs of realization include first of all the awareness of a radical shift of identity and understanding. The shift has a weight of authority that cannot be touched or approached by anything else. Also, the change must include both identity and understanding. Although it brings a degree of wonder and bewilderment, it is made of a vast clarity and direct insight. Whereas previously we understood spiritual teachings partially or vaguely, both the reality itself and the words that point to it are now crystal clear. If there is not the sense of thorough liberation and illumination, it is not realization.

The next sign is a great peace of mind, a peace that is weightless and transparent. This comes with a sense of release and lightness of heart that are too fine and subtle for words. It is not just that "I" am free but that reality is and has ever been free. Existence is whole, complete, and radiant. It was never the somewhat sad and senseless thing we imagined.

The next sign is the arising of a great love for all beings, almost like a slow-moving tidal wave. The tidal wave does not come to crash over and change and fix everyone like the restless waves of the deluded, missionary mind. It comes as a welling up of compassion, affection, and the awareness of inseparability. If this seeing is true, it brings an abiding urge to serve, help, and embrace others in truth and love.

All things become dear and precious, and that leads to the next sign, which is that for the awakened mind the preciousness of things and of human existence is not separate from but is rather a perfect reflection of the absolute. Though there is great detachment—a detachment made of total clarity as to the nature of delusion versus wisdom—there is no distance. The detachment is the clarity aspect of wisdom. The lack of distance is the love aspect of wisdom. So one feels the whole of the human experience as infinitely precious and meaningful, at the same time as knowing that our journey in life has been largely shaped by confusion. But we can awaken, and there are no mistakes in this divine scheme. There is only grace, and life is a precious opportunity to discover this.

By contrast, in the case of a shallow or partial insight, there is a characteristic, deluded idea that absolute truth or awareness stands apart from the relative facts, actions, and things of life. Being stuck in this view has been called being "stuck in the absolute" or being "stuck in emptiness," but ironically, it signifies precisely that one has not truly realized emptiness or the absolute. True, absolute emptiness voids the mind of every sense of separateness—including most of all the idea that the absolute and relative aspects of reality are separate.

The sum of these signs of genuine seeing is represented eventually by a clear, ordinary, and wise expression of truth and love within and through the human personality.

The years that followed awakening brought great change and adjustment. It was not all easy or smooth, but it was always filled with grace and wonder. There is a saying that today's enlightenment is tomorrow's mistake. Enlightenment does not make the human mind perfect. What it does reveal is the perfection of imperfection, and that is no small thing.

Awakening did not immediately remove every shade of suffering and confusion from my mind, but it did radically change the context and nature of the suffering. Even as I experienced emotional pain and obvious delusion at times, I could not entirely identify with any of it.

Difficulties continued to appear for me and were necessary for further purifying the mind and humbling the personality. I took responsibility for whatever was happening in life without identifying with it. I realized deeply that on the human level there is constant learning and change, and that life works to test, clarify, and strengthen one's realization of truth.

I would now say there is no quality more necessary in life than humility. Humility is a circle that holds all that we are—all that we know and do not know. Realizing the scope and infinity of the circle is enlightenment. Living in the wholeness of the circle is humility, humor, and compassion.

5

Life in Freedom

Give up your time, give up your life.
Give up the dream of not doing the laundry.
Do it, fold it while it's warm, and rejoice.

Now you are free for the evening, and love
starts making little movements of liberation
and chains start breaking for the joy of that motion.

Like chains dragging chains we struggle
and hurt too much, so let's drop the whole
weary business of holding on and holding out.

Carrying things around makes us tired and dull,
but the free giving away of everything we have and are
is the flight of a thousand cranes over the wide sea.

It is a slow beating of great white wings
by which we carry the last of our darkness
to the uproarious blaze of dawn.

Enlightenment is both an end and a beginning, just as when a refugee first stands within the border of a new land. The crossing marks the end of a core belief, the paradigm of division.

The hallmark of the shift is that we no longer identify with the mind-made self or mind stuff in general. What we experience instead is the absolute self of pure consciousness. As compared with the historical, mental self we once believed ourselves to be, this consciousness is *no-self*. It is empty of self-concepts but full of awareness and intelligence.

Do the enlightened claim to have arrived at an ultimate state or end point? This question comes from the divided mind. According to the divided mind, one is either in an incomplete state of imperfection or in an ultimate state of perfection. In this dualistic view, enlightenment is imagined as the perfection of personality, if not its complete nullification. We then see our own imperfect personality and use the imperfections to prove both that "I am not yet enlightened," and that "Anyone who claims enlightenment is claiming perfection."

In this case, the statement "I am not enlightened" is true in the relative sense but not for the imagined reason. The lack of enlightenment lies not in the imperfect personality or bad habits, but in the identification of self with the personality (habits of mind). When this identification is broken, we realize our essence beyond the habits. And then habits do change to a great degree.

Our problem is not with imperfection but with the failure to perceive the reality beyond perfection and imperfection. Enlightenment is not about becoming anything other than what you are. Reality is reality. There is no ultimate state. There is only waking up to what is. We already exist in and as the one reality of consciousness—we just don't know it. Once we know it, life goes on but is changed by that knowing. There is a deep okayness to things as they are.

Our concern with superiority and inferiority, perfection and imperfection, causes us to either idealize or devalue the possibility of enlightenment. We might want enlightenment so that we can become superior, or we might resent the idea that someone else is enlightened and that we are not. Meanwhile, the substance of enlightenment is simply to know that nothing and no one is separate; all apparent selves are only the one reality. This understanding amounts to existential sobriety.

According to Buddhist and other traditional descriptions, initial enlightenment knocks out the main pillars of ignorance, making way for further refinement. Once realized, the basic clarity of consciousness works to refine itself over time.

Even though it can always be said that everything is already whole and complete as it is—which we now understand—this view should not be used to deny the relative expression of wisdom and kindness versus delusion and conflict in human existence. Such denial is one of the age-old fixations of enlightenment sickness. To get stuck in enlightenment sickness means ultimately to lack the full fruit of enlightened wisdom.

The Zen tradition calls these people "elevated dead people," meaning, zombies. It would have been better that they remained ordinary humans with common sense and courtesy than to walk around spouting lifeless spiritual truisms. When spoken from fixation, even words about absolute truth are delusion. No one can argue with words that are superficially true but what matters most is how, why, and when they are spoken.

In today's enlightenment arena there are awakened people who are called "speakers." They speak truths, but do they teach and guide from a place of full insight and compassion? The Buddha, and Christ as well, was known for his ability to give teachings tailored to all levels of understanding. To one person he might say, "Meditate every morning," while to an advanced seeker he might say, "There is neither meditation nor anyone to meditate."

Once, after a talk when I had given various forms of guidance to people, a woman approached me and said, "I prefer the radical teaching that there is no person who needs any help." Note, however, that such a preference would not be spoken by someone who had actually realized emptiness. From the point of view of true emptiness, teachings addressed to different levels of understanding would be entirely appropriate. After all, there is no problem with people apparently needing a form of guidance, since all is empty. We must realize that to prefer or insist on only absolute teachings is one of the last and perhaps greatest delusions we can suffer.

If anything, the awakened one becomes more keenly aware of negative habits and distortions than ever. The first few years after my own shift were marked by rapid deconstruction of mind patterns. Though I no longer identified entirely with them, there was the unavoidable awareness that these patterns were still present and operative.

This fact was initially disturbing. I felt helpless as I observed or acted out mind states that I knew were not the truth. My own teacher had said, "You will not be able to control this." And it was true. There was no control at all. It is almost like being a child again.

Awareness became sensitive to the subtlest movement of thought, feeling, or sensation. This meant that the residual fixations quickly drew the corrective light of awareness. The post-awakening process also brought shifting states of awe, ecstatic weeping, extreme detachment, inflation, and bewilderment. There were many episodes when, touched by some small reflection of beauty or love, I would soon begin to sob uncontrollably; heart stricken and mind suspended by an unbearable and immense poignancy of divine love.

In such moments I found a spontaneous prayer emerging for all beings to know true love, and to be and feel loved. In the clarity of that blinding love I cared nothing for my own pains and troubles and prayed only to be of service.

The need for solitude, rest, and quiet contemplation was also very strong. In time the intensity of these states passed. It helped that I did not make a big deal out of tears, bliss, or intense feelings. Any fascination or preference for special states of mind gradually disappeared. The clarity born of awakening was doing its work, making everything equal in its sight.

The more lucidly aware you are, the less you get caught in mind and therefore the less you experience the weight of time. In former years there would be a gap of minutes, hours, or even days before I realized how the mind's stream of almost imperceptible thoughts and reactions had been stirring up worry or conflict. Now, awareness of these dynamics was immediate.

In this transparency of mind, stuckness and disturbance came and went more quickly. For example, if anger arose, then the sadness that might be behind the anger would quickly surface and dissolve the anger. Tears would rise up and flow in a bout of spontaneous release for a few minutes. I would feel the sadness as a raw energy moving through, free of any belief or narrative. The psyche was being fully released and emptied.

This releasing process is the exact inverse of feeling full of emotion, with a big story to go with it, yet being somehow unable to cry or let it through. The feeling is that something is coming through that you can neither stop nor hold onto. This is how a healthy psyche functions. It feels everything fully but nothing sticks.

In some cases, the energy of anger or sadness would operate for me like an intelligent alarm system, indicating something that was indeed off about a situation or interaction. By noticing the disturbance and just being curious about what it was showing, an insight would soon arise and the situation would right itself.

By the virtue of this process I eventually entered the quintessential, sublimely ordinary experience of liberation. No longer disoriented and overwhelmed by the energetic shock of awakening, the mind became stable, spacious, bright, and functional — its true nature.

Whereas awakening first created the sense of a brilliant white light of awareness that engulfed and nullified the human personality for a time, it now made itself at home in that structure, cleared it out and — finding no separation between the particular and the universal — manifested a more golden light of wholeness. It was as if the energetic radiance of consciousness were now resting in the heart and inhabiting my bones instead of bubbling upward and outward in the initial release from illusion.

Daily life took on a delightful simplicity and freshness. I especially enjoyed the sense of physical vitality. With the egoic mind no longer present as a dividing line or middleman between consciousness and nature, I experienced a palpable sense of oneness with the natural world.

I recall a solitary hike I took one misty California morning. I left an open area and entered a narrow valley with green hills on all sides. Blue jays darted through the mist, and in the silence I could hear water running somewhere far down below. I found a way to climb down the hillside, a descent through the brush that took about ten minutes.

When I reached the bottom I found a narrow crystal stream swiftly running over some rocks to a little waterfall and pool below, before it disappeared under the overhanging trees. Upon seeing this stream came tears of wonder and gratitude. This was not a case of emotionalizing over nature's beauty, which was not my habit to do. Prior to any thought, the sight of the stream instantly struck my consciousness as a symbol of spirit.

In such moments, consciousness, energy, and the natural world manifest their unity in an experience of joy. The observer and observed are one. Together, spirit and matter comprise the sacred, eternal world of creation. The creation is now, not before. Now is the first day of creation. This morning is the first morning, if we will learn to be born anew each day.

Life refreshes and renews us all the time unless we block it by clinging to the old. We cling to security which is only stagnation. Action always clears the stuck energy, and we have to learn to let decisions and actions arise and move through. For example, staying with a person who is completely wrong for us is not a sign of wisdom but rather of attachment and fear.

We should not get stuck in the idea that peace means not doing anything. Peace allows the right decision and action to happen more easily. Without the old unconscious resistances, I found that my actions were more spontaneous. Tasks that used to seem overwhelming and time-consuming were begun with boldness and enthusiasm.

Energy flowed into new areas of life. I found a new appreciation for color, design, and spatial arrangement and how these affect the mind. All aspects of life came into fuller color.

Moving energy every day became important. I continued to practice yoga and I took up road cycling. This allowed me to release great amounts of energy while exploring the rural roads of California or France.

For me cycling became a metaphor for the liberated life. Life in freedom is above all simple, running on natural power and inspiration. When you are on two wheels and gravity wants to pull you to one side or the other, you balance the tension of this duality by moving energy forward. Similarly, the surface duality of life is only a problem if we fixate and obstruct the flow. Then we collapse to one side.

We cannot find balance by refusing to move, waiting for the perfect moment, the perfect diet, or the perfect partner. We balance by moving with the flow, always being ready to adjust and adapt. When the mind is free of fixation we move intuitively and purposefully in life. We harmonize the polarity of opposites by objectively seeing what the moment asks for.

In egoic consciousness, what confuses our work and relationships is that we do not understand the fundamentals of the situation. We are adding so many superfluous demands and assumptions that we cannot possibly honor the situation for what it is. Fundamental principles include: There is a proper way to treat your parents; there is a proper approach to a first date; there are appropriate boundaries in a friendship, and so forth. When we ignore the basic principles for living (dharma), we make a mess of our lives and our minds remain disturbed. We cannot then expect to leap into the flow of oneness. We have to establish the ground of insight and equanimity.

Once we clarify the mind and dissolve the separative sense of self, things become infinitely more clear and simple. When you are cycling or engaged in a similarly absorbing activity, you are serenely alert, aware, and responsive with a minimum amount of mental chatter. Often people think that awakening will remove every trace of reflection from the mind; that they will function like a robot without any thinking at all.

In the clarity I am describing, there is thought and responsiveness to situations but without a self-image at the center of it. Awareness responds and reflects through the intellect. It is not a state of literally knowing nothing or being absolutely indifferent. We know what we need to know, when we need to know it.

Awareness shows us the big picture while also respecting the relevant facts of the moment. When we lack consciousness we cannot see the whole. Therefore the mind is easily taken over by an archetype or extreme of some kind, to the exclusion of all other possibilities.

What we call unconsciousness or egoic consciousness is essentially a condition of possession and dissociation. When you are possessed by a certain idea, identity, or opinion, this of course means a dissociation from other possibilities or realities. Egoic consciousness is above all a state of being possessed by the idea that reality is a problem to be fixed—usually by introducing some degree of force or violence against oneself or others.

Egoic thinking never appreciates the spontaneous, intelligent movement in consciousness toward order and self-actualization—both in oneself and in society. It sees its own authoritarian voice as the savior of self or humanity. *"You need me,"* says the devilish voice of ego, *"for without me you will never be powerful, safe, or successful. Let me organize your life for you, and also the lives of others for that matter."* Anyone who challenges this doctrine is viewed as dangerous or irresponsible.

In liberation, the drive to fix oneself or others is recognized as an adolescent dream, a zealot's obsession. The great mythologist Joseph Campbell said, *"Instead of clearing his own heart, the zealot tries to clear the world."* A zealot is one who thinks reality is broken.

When the mind falls into one-sided views, all happiness and wholeness are forced out of view, and the mind is charged with the incredible tension of being split. The mind in this condition cannot know anything real and cannot know happiness.

Happiness is the experience of consciousness reflecting within a clear mind. Happiness is not in things. Happiness is in the wholeness of things.

Liberated consciousness is simply happy, and that is my experience. I know what it is like to be lost in the mind's miscreations and to feel life as a burden. And I know what it means to discover life as grace. One who is free wants to share this freedom with others.

Life is communication. The real goal of communication is to commune. Spiritual teaching is a communication that works to remove the primary block to communion, our deluded thinking.

When a human being experiences herself or himself as separate and disempowered, it is not because of a complicated psychological issue or energetic imbalance. It is because of false beliefs that pile up into false identity.

We can sort through the mess of these beliefs and feelings, looking for healing like a needle in a haystack, or we can learn to consistently step back, observe the whole picture and see it as false. That total seeing, at the level of identity, is the end of the disempowerment. There is no substitute for that understanding. Everything else is a belief in some magical process that will somehow fix what was never broken.

Like other forms of teaching, spiritual teaching thrives in a spirit of friendship and equality. Equality does not mean to pretend that everyone's views and actions are equally wise and beautiful. Those who have understood the difference between wisdom and delusion, love and fear, feel responsible for helping others reach the same.

This is not the kind of responsibility assumed by the divided mind. It is more so a natural response to the human experience, and I have known few greater joys than helping others to claim a life of love and freedom for themselves.

I emphasize that I do not teach anything new, and my experience is not special. The universal teaching is that our real nature is unconditioned, eternally pure and one with all things. Our thoughts, feeling, and actions are shaped by contact with this reality or the lack of it.

Awakening points to a radical change of heart. Heart is a metaphor for our moral sensitivity and feeling. If your understanding is clear it gives birth to a love and devotion that never tires of its own humility before the mystery of life and God. The more true wisdom shines through a human mind, the more humility will be there.

When the heart and mind have been transformed by acquainting with the unconditioned, the origin, then we say I love *It*, the formless unfathomable divine, and I love you, the embodied beings and creatures of the earth. I love you as you really are. I love you even if you are confused or frightened or obnoxious. I am always here for you in the deepest sense. I can never abandon you because I am you.

None of us can be all things to all people, but spiritually we live with the feeling of devotion to the well-being of all. With this feeling we serve life in whatever way comes to us to serve. We all serve. The animals and trees serve. Even the stones are serving. They remind us there is a deeper way to listen.

Through the love of truth I have been made simple. I do not want any power other than to love, to understand, and to inspire. What is left when the belief in separation is gone? Silence, speech, movement, touch. Humanity, divinity. All the same.

Yet this is not a state of stagnation. It is the creative poise of consciousness. It is a condition like being in love—timeless yet in tune, fulfilled by little things because one has found the beloved.

We have all experienced simple, divine moments. In such moments the mind is relatively clear and consciousness is sensitized to itself. We can then feel the basic sanity of our being. What would it be like to live every moment from this lucid and empowered point of view, freely listening, receiving, and responding to life?

The only thing that can bring such constancy is a full shift of values and identity. We start by examining the value we have placed in the false. By learning to discern and value truth, we awaken in truth.

To ask about the role of values in enlightenment is like asking about the role of chocolate in making a chocolate cake. A value is what you see as meaningful and desirable to you. We all value happiness while undervaluing its source.

To awaken means to refine and revolutionize our values in the emergent light of awareness. As the false self is made of nothing other than false values, a shift in what we value will automatically create a shift of identity. In this rebirth I become what I am, I love what is, and I do what happens.

Reality is good. We are always saved by the fact that reality is reality, that the artifice of illusions, no matter how convincing, has chinks in it through which truth enters. In every difficult moment there is an opening. That opening is God's eye in your life. And when you open to your true nature, then your whole life begins to function as God's eye in the world.

Being God's eye in the world is a universal calling. And the good news is that you already have everything you need to fulfill this calling. You are the light of world. Your sole task is to accept this fact and the life it reveals to you.

6

Originality

If you want to come alive then you must become original. Originality comes from knowing the origin. To be original means to acquaint with consciousness, the stillness beneath the masks and identities we wear. This brings freshness and authenticity of being.

To come to the origin is a labor of love. And love's first task is to see where you are unconscious and untruthful in your life. By courageously investigating the false we trigger vast changes within. With the constant exercise of discernment we learn to bring the light of truth to each situation instead of repeating the past. We then feel as though more and more light is coming into the mind until at last we awaken as that light—beyond mind, beyond all the sorrows of the past.

To meet each other here is the fulfillment we seek. Go there yourself and the others will be there. A new life will come. But first you must go. There is no other way and no one else who can do this but you.

Of course, either you are motivated to know and live the truth or not. There is no blame in not wanting to know, though there are consequences in your experience. Many who say they want to awaken do not yet have fidelity or passion for this inner process. What they want is to feel better, to cling to their habits and hope that realization lands on their doorstep one day.

For example, we might think to ourselves something like this: "Okay, I will consent to meditate every day. If I don't start feeling wonderful very soon then I will know I've been lied to." Their bargaining indicates that the passion for truth and the simple desire to come home to themselves has not arisen in their experience. By contrast, those who are called to awaken can think of nothing else and gladly plunge into their own depth like someone dying of thirst dives into a river.

Once it awakens in you the spiritual urge drives everything. There comes a willingness to know the truth and to let it have its way in your life at all cost. We do not know what the cost is beforehand in terms of changes that may arise when we reach a new level of integrity and insight, but we are inevitably freed by the changes. So the cost is really nothing, and the gain is every-thing.

We can do this the hard way, which means long suffering and dissatisfaction brought by compromise, or we can go the swift way of integrity. When a change in our lives comes from truth then it will be seen that whatever happens is right and good, even if it is difficult. If it is a broken heart, then it will serve its true purpose—of breaking the heart open forever and evolving the consciousness of real love. The fruit of the lesson or the loss is always a deeper love and freedom of being.

Suffering drives us to wake up, but suffering itself is not the lesson. When suffering goes on and on, that is actually the refusal of the lesson. We do not wake up merely by suffering. We wake up by bringing our suffering to light. The light of conscious presence always cancels the heaviness of repetition and time, returning us to our timeless nature, where we register a sense of flow and lightness.

The place where this correction happens is right here in our life circumstances. As integrity grows our lives become a more faithful reflection of the truth. As you clarify your mind you will have strong intuitions of spirit, moments of spaciousness and joy that arise on their own. Know that this is the fragrance of your true nature. Allow yourself to embrace this real life, the truth that you love.

In that wholehearted embrace your arms will be forced to drop the other things you are carrying. When the love of truth reaches sufficient intensity it sets your gaze on the highest happiness. Love will then appear or function as the dynamic intelligence that burns away attachment to all that is less than your true nature—the substitute satisfactions that have always disappointed.

Until your love of truth reaches that level of intensity, your attention is split and your freedom appears to be elusive. Yet freedom, love, and truth are not elusive. They shine forth in plain sight when you are finished with hiding from yourself.

Do not get caught in thinking it takes a lot of time to awaken. Awakening is the overthrow of time and everything you think time requires. Your reality is timeless and there lies your power to recognize it, now. This very moment is a powerful ally, always inviting you into a more vivid and integral life.

There comes a time to rise boldly out of a certain smallness of mind and trivial way of living. The fundamental human desire is to live and to give from our real nature. Acknowledging and fulfilling this desire is the only way to liberate our minds from the tyranny of fear.

By nurturing this one desire and bearing its immensity, reactive emotions coalesce into a steady stream of devotion. Reactive emotion is love that has not yet been made conscious. A focus on truth makes love conscious and dissolves emotional reactivity.

On the strength of that focus the mind becomes stable and clear. Thus the cure for anxiety, despair, and a hundred little worries is not to forcibly train the mind to be quiet. The cure is to align ourselves with our ultimate purpose. Through that alignment the mind and body begin to work as a channel for life-giving energy and thought.

In other words, to arrive in peace you must go by way of passion. The passion of spirit to know itself is unique because instead of seeking to add something to ourselves it empties us. As soon as we are sufficiently empty of the world, life rushes in. Life is not the world. The mental, man-made world of cynicism, delusion, and denial is an overlay upon life and the natural world. But the incoming light of consciousness shows us a new heaven and earth, and brings the mind into divine simplicity.

It is said that God rushes into a pure soul as quickly as light pours in through a window. What makes the soul pure? Love of truth. Love of truth removes distorted views and reveals right values, values that make the mind fresh and buoyant.

Look deeply at your habits and lifestyle. If there is a sincere desire to know the truth of your being then consciousness will ensure that your life is aligned with that. Consciousness will direct the mind to make certain changes. Each increase in integrity and insight will lead to the next.

Clarifying the mind is the sole task of the seeker. If the mind is disturbed, some insights may come but they will not transform. All disturbances are a sign of false beliefs and values that are still operating. If your mind retains false values you will only have the skin of freedom, not the bones. It's the skin that talks. Bones walk. Until you get the bones, you cannot stand truly free. But when love of truth is in your bones and the mind is emptied of the false, then you stand, you walk, you dance in that freedom.

7

Outshining Ignorance

From horizon to horizon
a strange noise is bounding.
Thunder, it is thunder you say,
for you are older now, you know
the name of this sound.
Rain has been coming steady
while you sleep, surrounded
by your dream.

Think you that you know
what thunder is, and rain,
because you have names?
Yet you can hardly say what it means
to wake in the night and listen,
suddenly so nakedly alone
in your senses,
rapt beyond all reason.

You know then the great silent thing
that empties you between each rumbling—
You are not what you think,
nor the world what it appears.

As consciousness is unchanging, enlightenment is not, strictly speaking, a process of altering, increasing, or expanding consciousness. It is a process of subtracting ignorance.

When a thick layer of clouds dissolves, we can see and feel the sun that was always shining behind them. Yet the sun never changed. The turning of the earth brings a new morning and the apparent rising of the sun. In the same way, when we turn our attention toward our true nature, the felt presence of awareness seems to appear anew. Of course it has always been there, but our attention was directed elsewhere.

By turning the light of attention upon itself, awareness seems to grow and expand. Its presence feels more lucid, rich, and vast. Thoughts receive less fuel and slow down. The neutral space of stillness allows the mind to relax and may catalyze a powerful release of emotion, energy, laughter, or mystic visions and insights. Yet nothing is being added to us. No matter how dramatic the mind states are, it is only the impact of shedding ignorance.

Spiritual ignorance does not imply a lack of intelligence. Ignorance is simply the condition of ignoring or not being aware of the actual nature of reality. When we have never heard of enlightenment, we tend to see the symptoms of ignorance as unavoidable. We fail to appreciate that we are suffering the effects of basic, pervasive delusion. Ignorance can therefore be likened to being lost without knowing you are lost.

This type of lostness only reveals itself through increasing struggle and bewilderment. Eventually we grasp that we are suffering because of a fundamental confusion about life that we have never dealt with. Knowing we are existentially lost can be called the beginning of the spiritual search. We can also see that this search has always been with us, albeit in an unconscious mode.

The search for fulfillment is built into the struggle and process of human life. Right from the beginning, we misidentify our being and our happiness with external things and circumstances. We cannot help this. Many substitutes for truth are accepted along the way, and substitutes always lead to disillusionment. This is the natural process of growing up.

The real meaning of growing up is to become conscious, an awake being. We become conscious through the dynamic of identifying ourselves with something only to later disidentify and realize a new wholeness and independence from that thing, activity, or situation. To outgrow something means consciousness got tired of identifying with something less than its own fullness and potential.

We outgrow not only interests and activities but entire paradigms and modes of being. When the defining theme or logic of a developmental phase has fulfilled itself, its main limitation is revealed and becomes increasingly uncomfortable to live with. The mind endures instability and uncertainty as it seeks its next foothold.

From birth onward we move through stages of unconscious identification, discomfort, and disidentification. This is the game of consciousness played out in each individual mind. The toys of childhood give way to the more sophisticated amusements of adulthood. Whereas the play of childhood was spontaneous and vital for learning, our adult games often continue long after the joy of discovery has passed.

When disillusionment continues into adulthood without revealing a new horizon of discovery, it is easy to rationalize that this must be all that life offers. If we do not break new ground of wisdom we easily fall into the trap of cynicism and despair. Perhaps we expected that growing up would lead easily to wisdom, but instead of shedding our illusions we find we have only exchanged the simple illusions of childhood for more complex ones.

The game of realizing wholeness is still on, but as life presents us with seemingly unsolvable riddles and contradictions it may seem like senseless torment. Not knowing where to find clarity, we develop conflicted, chattering minds distracted by the routines and amusements of materialism. Eventually, our basic ignorance catches up with us and triggers a crisis of some kind.

The spiritual game is serious, although its goal is the revelation of lightness. We could say that in its quest to actualize the infinite lightness of its own being, consciousness makes the ignorance feel heavier and heavier.

According to the materialistic outlook, we just have to add more novelty and spice to our lives to maintain the façade of being fulfilled by things and experiences. Enlightenment offers an entirely different possibility. We can wake up out of the game of identity.

This is the last disillusionment, the final frontier, and what a refreshing vista it presents. At last, consciousness uses the mind to question the primal sense of separateness. At this juncture we realize that gaining new and better experiences cannot add anything to us. We can accept and enjoy positive experiences but we no longer expect them to deliver lasting peace and fulfillment. As our understanding becomes more sharp and subtle, we lose interest in the identity project that has been driving us our entire life.

When our mental and emotional energy no longer fuels the restless distraction and seeking of the separative mind, the mask of persona has no support and crumbles. We no longer know who we are. We find it difficult to sustain the image we and others have had of ourselves. Our former vanity and self-absorption are exchanged for transparent authenticity. We cease to live for the story we are telling, preferring life in its raw immediacy.

The sense of self is a process defined by the movement and investment of energy. It becomes very shaky in moments of neutrality and stillness. Such moments are typically felt as an intolerable emptiness and boredom, to be quickly escaped. But when consciousness is ready to know itself, we will be helpless and unable to direct attention away from the truth. The seemingly awful truth we are being forced to confront is actually love—not the image we have made of love, but love actually. Real love is unconditional because its nature is empty, free of conditions.

The quality of having one's mental-emotional energy

suspended and nullified is the experience of death. All death is psychological. Death is the absence of any experience or object to cling to. It is the agonizing inner voidness of loss. It is primal uncertainty and destabilization.

Sure, you see the room full of familiar objects around you, but when you are psychologically removed from them, your surroundings cease to bring you the familiar comfort and security. You are not going crazy, you are going sane. Consciousness is having its day, but what is day to consciousness is experienced as night for our long-held ignorance. The soul, consciousness, does not go through a dark night—only our ignorance does.

The purpose of death is not to end life and bring a new one. It is to reveal eternal life, the timeless. When you move through the final threshold and outgrow all mind-made identities, you are reborn in spirit. Of course, this is what you have always been. Pure being, pure awareness, pure knowing. Then you live the divine game as consciousness itself. You have always been one with life, but now you know it. Having outshined the former ignorance, you are now just the shining.

8

Consciousness

If you hear music
floating out from somewhere
then it is God's music
and it is God who listens.

But if you see the musician
then you think again in terms
of separate identities.

This thought craze make us talk nonsense
about proving whether a thing like God exists
when the fact is nothing exists as a thing
but all things are the song of an empty
and total radiance.

When the mask of separate identity
happens to slip off your stifled head,
then music floats out from nowhere
and God starts dancing everywhere.

Everyone experiences a mind and a body. What is less obvious is the true nature of mind and body. Usually we do not imagine that there is such a thing as true nature. We tend to think that how we experience our selfhood is precisely how it is, though in the back of our minds we have a nagging doubt. This doubt is what saves us.

When we derive our identity from mental contents and body image we entertain a delusion of great proportions. Though we recognize that our mind is often filled with dissatisfaction, fear, and frustration, we are generally unaware of the cause. We do not realize that we are experiencing the symptoms of mistaken identity.

Our delusion is all the more pernicious because we can scarcely conceive that we are ensnared in it. Despite all the misery it creates, our identification with mind patterns as who and what we are feels entirely convincing and normal. It has been said that no one is so hopelessly enslaved as one who falsely believes himself to be free. This is our human condition. It is a twilight dream-state, filled with shifting inner scenes and moods that torment us for their lack of a reliable touchstone of truth.

The metaphors of sleep, dream, and darkness have long been used to describe humanity's unconscious state. They also hint at our capacity to awaken and enlighten. Our nature is the light. Our freedom, for better or worse, is to misuse this light to create false beliefs and live in the shadows they cast, with all the difficulty that entails. Our freedom is also to withdraw these projected shadows back into the light of reality that we are.

I often use the word twilight to describe the human condition because it is not a state of absolute darkness. It does contain some light. Just as twilight requires a measure of light, a dream requires a measure of reality.

During a dream, the aspect that is real is you, the dreamer. Your consciousness powers the dream-state. It does not matter how helplessly lost you seem to get in the dream story, for it is not your nature to sleep and dream forever. The same consciousness that creates the dream is also capable of awakening out of it.

It is the same in the waking state. We are the conscious presence behind the outward display of life, but we do not appreciate the depth and power of our conscious nature. In the unawakened state of mind, we tend to see our consciousness as something like a solitary, 40-watt light bulb flickering and buzzing in a dim and cluttered little room of mind. This little light appears to turn on in the morning and fade away at night into the oblivion of sleep.

In fact our consciousness is more like the sun that is lighting up the whole world. Open the window, peer outside the cramped little room of mind and see it's a glorious day outside. There is a fresh and timeless sense of presence wafting into the long-stifled room. It seems to come from somewhere far beyond you, yet it is your own nature. This silent blessing speaks to a place in us beyond our sophisticated defenses and rationalizations. It speaks of innocence, of knowing, and of freedom from every kind of narrowness.

This is the opening to consciousness as it really is. Yet we cry out in despair saying, *"Please can I just have a little bit of light!"* Why is it so difficult to know and enjoy the light, direct? We experience a veil. The entire history of humanity is this veil; the shadows and uncertainties it creates and the brief, glorious moments of transparency, mercy, and redemption.

Due to our apparent separateness from the grace of spirit, it seems that a bit of light and love have to descend on us from above or beyond us. But the veil is self-created. Though we cannot expect to remove the veil instantly, we can begin by examining our assumptions about what we are and why we experience separation. It may be that the veil is only made of assumptions that we make again and again without being aware of other possibilities.

The question of what our nature is, and what the veil might be, must begin with a clear look at the basic facts of our experience. We start with the epistemological question of how we know anything, including our own existence. Here we can acknowledge that consciousness is the power by which we are aware of anything at all, and by which we know that we exist. It is impossible to deny the presence of awareness and thus existence. I am aware, therefore I am.

So, to exist is to be conscious. You may be tempted to say that you exist because you have a body, but without consciousness you would know nothing of a body. A body without consciousness is said to be a dead body.

We tend to assume that consciousness is a product of the brain or body. This belief is due to sensory hypnosis combined with pseudoscientific rationalism. We have all been hypnotized by our senses since childhood. As so much attention goes into using our senses to navigate the world, we come to identify completely with their functioning.

The senses function through the body, so it feels as though the body is the awareness that receives sensory input, as in the statement, "My body hears, my body sees, my body feels." Yet to be more accurate, we have to say that all sense perception is received by the abstract quality called awareness, not by the body.

Though we might say, "My ears hear," it is consciousness that receives and knows the sound, not ears. Ears are the mechanism by which sound is received in awareness. Eyes are the mechanism by which things are seen in awareness. Even when we close all the senses down, as in a sensory deprivation tank, awareness remains.

Awareness is prior to both the senses and the mind because it is their knower. For example, you have seen your eyes, but your eyes have never seen you. You have observed thoughts coming and going, but thoughts have never observed you. You have commanded your arms and legs to move, but your arms and legs have never moved you.

What is this "you" that observes? Anything you can point to in the world or in your mind is secondary to your awareness of it. Therefore, no observable thing defines you. That includes the thoughts and moods that arise and take hold of your identity for a while. They shape your experience for a while but they do not mean anything about who and what you really are.

The reason we overlook our essential, conscious nature is that it defies objectification. It is ungraspable by the senses or intellect which we use for everything else. The senses are adequate for distinguishing water from wine, and the intellect is adequate for explaining what makes them different, but neither the senses nor the intellect can capture the consciousness that precedes them. This is not a problem, however, because consciousness already knows itself.

Being pure, self-reflective intelligence, consciousness does not need to reject the sensory world or intellect to know itself—it needs only to spontaneously contemplate its own nature with a bit of help from the intellect with which it is identified. The intellect's role in this is only to formulate the initial, verbal question: *What am I?*

This question turns attention away from all the external objects that the senses and intellect are usually occupied with and onto the light of self. What, then, is this consciousness that knows its own presence?

We cannot say in objective terms what consciousness is, but why should we expect to do so? To be objective means to objectify, yet that only works when dealing with objects. For example, we can say that a jar is made of glass, a table is made of wood, or that water consists of hydrogen and oxygen, but we cannot say what consciousness is made of. We can only say that it exists.

Unlike everything else, consciousness is not a separate object or thing. It is not composed of something other than itself. That is why we say that consciousness is absolute reality. What is absolute is defined as indivisible and not composed of parts. Thus to be objective about consciousness means to recognize that it cannot be objectified.

When we recognize that our nature cannot be captured as an object, we enter the domain of non-duality where all questions about self dissolve into one wordless, living answer. Given that the things we see and touch cannot tell us about the meaning, nature, and significance of our existence, it is often said that there are no answers to these deep questions. Yet the problem lies with our concept of what an answer would look like; the form it would arrive in.

Words like "To get to London, take this road" are concrete, easily received and utilized. In this case, the words effectively divide the right way from the wrong way. Words about identity and essence tend to imply divisions that do not apply. For example, words like awareness, self, and love seem to imply separate qualities or emotions, but in direct experience they all belong to the same reality of our nature—like different facets of the same diamond, or rainbow colors emerging from the one light as it passes through the diamond.

When we are sensitized to the wholeness of our conscious nature, we feel the meaning or poignancy of life direct—as the love, creativity, and wisdom that flows from conscious presence and which *is* that presence. Words in the form of spiritual teachings or poetic inspiration may have helped us discover that direct experience, but once the experience is realized we no longer rely on words or conceptual answers alone.

It is then obvious that those who are looking for answers exclusively within the mind, in conceptual structures, are partly right when they give up and declare that, "There are no answers." Yet they overlook the only thing, the only one, who could know and receive the answer as a direct experience. Consciousness is the answer, but it does not speak in the fragmented language of the intellect. It speaks in the language of totality. To learn that language is to know yourself.

9

Desire

There are two qualities that emerge as we clarify our nature—innocence and passion. The world thinks it knows innocence when it looks at a baby, but that knowledge of innocence is secondhand and indirect. The baby is innocent, at least for the time being, but we are not.

As the innocence of the baby is not conscious but is only a circumstance of not having lived here very long, it quickly becomes a child and then an adult who is neither conscious nor innocent. We do not know innocence until we have been made innocent again, by becoming conscious. To be innocent again means to be free of all the cynicism and false knowledge we accumulate as we grow up.

Similarly, the world thinks it knows passion in the form of sensory excitement and lust for experience. That passion is indirect and tainted by attachment and fear. Pure passion is when consciousness revels in its own stillness and beauty. This is registered in the mind as the knowledge, "I am the origin." Consciousness then sees all of creation arise in itself and loves the movement of life. But it registers that the ecstasy lies in the source of that movement and not just the outward appearance.

So in my original innocence and passion, I am free of the ignorance of depending on events for happiness. I no longer depend on festivals, sports, romance, tragedy, or political drama to feel vibrant and alive. Instead there is the deeper romance of life in depth, where I am the bringer of happiness to each situation or relationship.

I work, play, dance, or make love in joy. For I am pure again. I am creative in the deepest sense, without necessarily having to make or produce something.

Anything I make or produce—any work of art for example—cannot possibly be greater than its source and creator. The world always has it backwards, elevating the product over the creator, the observed over the observer. And that is why the worldly, extroverted mind becomes very tired. It chases objects and the shadows cast by objects instead of turning toward its own light. It lives in the thrall of spectacle and appearance.

As you realize innocence you enter a new life, or a new life grows out of the old. You will see that life follows an inner law and that in everything that matters you are divinely guided. You will know you never had to get rid of all desires, preferences, or thoughts. You only had strip the coarser illusions from them.

Desire is originally innocent but it gets corrupted by fear and grasping, so that we cannot receive anything real. When desire becomes demand, you may receive something but it will not be true and real. Most of all we demand love from others. They may seem to comply if they are afraid of the anger behind our demand, but we will not receive love through our demand. Love only comes to those who are nonviolent, who are unwilling to indulge the old emotional violence within them.

Desire, free of violence, is only joy that wants to share itself. All desires are the desire for reality, to communicate or share in presence. Desire is originally a river that flows toward the ocean of union. The problem is when the river gets blocked or sidetracked, forgetting its true aim. In the ocean of spirit all natural desires find their right proportion and are fulfilled. How these are fulfilled will surprise and delight you. You will feel your life flowing in a deep current of joy instead of splashing in the shallow puddles of contrived pleasures.

To purify the stream of desire you have to work with the energy of longing and the frustration of desire in yourself. Never block your desire. Never pretend it is not there. Instead admit that it is enormous.

You have seen those films where an ambitious person

confesses, "I want the whole world." That is how our desire really is. Not that we want to own the world, but what we want is total, absolute fulfillment. We want complete pleasure and ecstasy.

In childhood our desire begins as selfish, blind want for nourishment and enjoyment without much conscious concern for the other. We soon learn that, beyond the satisfaction of our physical needs, in order for our happiness to be complete then others must be included and considered. In this way our temporary shell of selfishness is gradually broken open by the social nature of life.

Our desire gets channeled more and more toward cooperative and constructive activities. To play the best games, we need playmates. To enjoy laughter we need another to share the hilarity of the moment. To weigh the full import of our thoughts and feelings we need someone to hear, understand, and reflect them back to us.

In relationship there is a balance of giving and receiving. We learn to receive pleasure from giving and to give pleasure by receiving. If someone refuses to take then your pleasure of giving is blocked. And if you refuse to receive love and affection then the other's pleasure is blocked along with the flow of spiritual energy that underlies it.

This applies to all relationships and encounters, however trivial they appear. So you have to become a vessel that can receive and give in the right way. This mainly plays out in the tasks of adult life as Freud named them: to love and to work. In the balance of giving and receiving our love and work become play; play which includes both exertion and rest. We are in the play and rhythm of life, which must alternate between action and inaction, thought and the absence of thought, community and solitude.

One who has realized life as play has taken his or her existence seriously enough to act on desires but intelligently so, letting them lead the way through and past the surface goal. A man initially wants a woman to sleep with, but with receptivity he allows himself to be led to a deeper experience of communication, perhaps the creation of a life together and all the growth this entails. And so his desire eventually reveals the spiritual communion and growth he initially sought in a body.

It leads him beyond the body, but if he refused to follow his body at all, attempting to make himself a saint, then he becomes a coward who is not only afraid of women, sex, and rejection but afraid of life. There is no way to leap from being a coward to a saint in one bound—one must at least become human first, through the courageous life of action and desire tempered by increasing wisdom.

Those who have not gone through the fires of their desire cannot find great peace; they will only find a small and static island of peace defended by repression. To earn peace you need to have come absolutely alive. You cannot have repression in your system. You have to have insisted on speaking and living in truth with others and not to settle for the great lie of appearances—the lie of the lifeless marriage, the dishonest friendships, or the hidden agony of living just to please others.

As the ancients said, if you cannot find good spiritual company in your land, then you must go into the desert. The desert offers us a metaphor. What will you find in the desert? Fire. Heat.

You will be alone, but the heat will help you dry up all the dampness in your soul and set your heart on fire with new life. If you live a water-logged, compromised, and emotionally stale life then you can never know fire and the great, clear space of peace that fire leaves when its work is done.

This is why I have said that if you want peace, you must go by way of passion. Passion is the drive of the great intelligence to fulfill itself in the human experience. No external thing or person can completely fulfill this, so even as you achieve a pleasurable life situation with a balance of giving and receiving, you are still left with a profound longing.

This is where passion turns inward, toward the infinite intelligence of spirit within, to discover vastness. By seeing through the idea of yourself as an object that can gain happiness from another object, you awaken as the life force of presence itself.

You go from being a small vessel to an all-embracing and all-giving vessel. You start to resonate with awakened presence, which people feel as an energetic balm or nectar emanating from you. This empty awakeness is a vital, flowing peace in which passion is constantly fulfilling itself in relation with the whole that is life.

Thus to think that we can or should cut off all desires from the start is a tragic error. It is the same as concluding that if certain negative thoughts cause suffering then freedom must mean not to have any thoughts. Our task is not to banish thoughts and desires but to enlighten them.

Ask yourself, do I suffer because I desire, or do I suffer because my desire and the vision behind my desires is not great enough, not powerful enough to lift me out of smallness and separateness? You may indeed have some anxious, misguided desires fueled by fear and lack. Go to their root. Gradually these can be converted to one great desire for love and truth that uplifts your life and the lives of others.

There is only one power in existence, and that is spirit. So you have to watch what you attempt to throw away or change in yourself. Hafiz said, *"Spare the world your ideas of good until you know that all is good."* It may be that your nagging, selfish desire or bad habit holds a great message within it. It is a vessel, albeit an inadequate vessel, for the urge to be happy and whole, to be nakedly revealed to yourself and others. That would be peace and that would be power.

When you want to awaken, you are going to need a great power, a great passion for truth and for life. How can you possibly receive the revelation of wholeness if you attempt to stifle your desire for happiness? You cannot get to the root of your being by cutting off your branches. You have to grow both upward into the world and downward into the unmanifest. This is the way of enlightening your desire for happiness.

10

Benediction

The moment when tears
are on their way
but not yet come.

The stirring of immeasurable depths
of sadness and love within.

The clouds each day this season
tell of tears on their way
as I witness the birth of this empty
and singing heart.

And if I begin to weep
for this world and all that's in it,
then I know the ecstatic weeping
of this surrendered soul
will never end.

Timeless love is breathing you now. It is the subtle air of our being. But we become hardened. When we are existentially numb we cannot feel, we cannot shed tears, but life will eventually break us open. When that time comes we find there are many tears to cry. Gradually these shift from being tears of helplessness and hopelessness to tears of love and of knowledge being born within.

It has been said that if you have not wept deeply you have not even begun to meditate. So we meditate on our suffering, and when we have cried enough tears of love—tears that leave the heart more empty and open to life—we find ourselves more and more at home in our being.

In this vastness and simplicity we may find ourselves often weeping for no particular reason. These are tears of emptiness. They are the ecstasy of a love that has no object and no end in sight. And these tears are the signs that true vision has come.

Vision is to see that this human life is a ship launched from the shores of the eternal. Each body will sail out, circle and return according to its own unique plan. Knowing that nothing is at stake in this voyage is a great relief. It is the reason we have been told that all is already forgiven.

When your essential worth and identity are no longer in question you can relax inside and enjoy the ride. You will not worry about death. When you deeply contemplate death, you realize death is already here. Death means we are already the vast self who was here before birth and who will also watch the body fall away.

It has been said that things teach best when they are dying. Death brings great love, because it shows us we have no power or substance other than the love, the consciousness, we are. Every other power we can imagine or wield for a time in this world will disappear and leave us empty. In that shocking emptiness we discover to what extent we have realized love as our nature.

If we live with this emptiness now, we bring real life to our living. Without the wisdom from death, life becomes fretful and constricting, like the politicians who say their job is to protect us and keep us secure. Whatever presumes to protect you robs you of life. Life is not for merely keeping the body alive for 100 years. The mind and body are protected in the deepest sense by the knowledge of their real purpose, which is to serve in consciousness.

The experience of being resolved to the higher purpose or process of things is called peace. Being resolved to the purpose of life makes us lighter, not heavier. It breaks up the atmosphere of tension in our lives. The tension is there between the parent and the child, when the parent rules with shame and control. It is there between a wife and husband, who have trouble discussing anything without turning it into a petty argument. It is there between teacher and student, when the teacher wields a curriculum of fear based on false standards of intelligence and learning.

Just behind this pretense of deadly seriousness, a great laughter awaits our discovery. It waits for us to relax out of our mental cramp and see things as they are. In this relaxation we see that nothing serious is actually happening. We are making the whole drama up, terrorizing ourselves for no good reason. This is a serious problem, and one that ends in laughter.

When you taste the truth and the world turns inside out in your vision, then you will laugh like you have never laughed. That laughter is within you now. It is a great, uproarious laughter because it has been held down so very long—because the truth is so radically different than our story about life.

Nothing announces your freedom like this laughter of emptiness. To hear this strange laughter rising from the depths of consciousness is the greatest wonder. When this laughter awakens in you, you will really know that you are free. You will own your independence as a free being on this planet, no longer subject to its destructive games of separation.

Love is the way to laughter and freedom. If you are not laughing often enough, it means you are out of touch with love. Be serious, if anything, about getting in touch with love, and then lightness will come.

Let your mind be still and free of worry. Look at what you are worried about—it comes down to love. Love would end the worry. Love ends all fear.

You have always done the best you could do. You will continue to do your best. Your increasing understanding of what is best brings all the qualities of your true nature to the fore, just as an ocean wave brings a crest of foam forward to crash into the shore. At that crest is the outward action and appearance of your life.

What gives the crest beauty and height is the silent, rising wave of spiritual understanding that grows within the contemplative mind. What is the contemplative mind? It is the mind that is set on the greatest love. It is inspired by love, it longs for love, and it finds that love because the human mind is born of love.

This love finds its foundation in humility, forgiveness, and simplicity. It is spontaneous compassion for every shadow of sorrow that darkens the face of humanity. Most importantly, this love is joy. It is happiness. It is certainty, not of some thing or outcome, but a certainty of being.

The mind will only rest upon the ground of this trust and joy in the truth. The invisible, living truth is what you love in every form. Truth is what liberates. And there is no other way of liberation than to sort out the true and the false right here within the mind's present dilemmas. God is found right in the place where God seems to be lost.

The vital question for us is, "Am I merely a thing or am I the ineffable, aware intelligence of spirit?" If you know your pure essence then you are free to be in the world but not of it. But if you believe that you are merely a thing, a creature, then the vastness of spirit remains hidden to you.

When we are lost in material identity, it is as if the sun had confused itself with one of its rays, and then further mistook itself for a mote of dust appearing within the ray. You are not a piece of dust on the earth. You are the light of consciousness.

Consciousness is the sun of spirit. It just sits there illumining and loving everything it beholds. The human intellect is the ray of light that can bounce around and reflect upon this or that. The earth and the body appear within this one light. As you are already the sun of existence, you can learn to recognize your own light. Speak love, invite love, and most of all give love, and its light will be reflected back to you with increasing intensity, until you have no doubt this is your real nature.

The ray of the mind, thought, will continue to move and play in the world, but its movement can be grounded in total clarity. As we attune to pure awareness, we gain the power to see through trivial thoughts or negative feelings on the spot. Instead of asking ourselves why there are still trivial or hostile thoughts arising in the mind, we can simply ignore such arisings and flick them off. We develop a sense of humor and forgiveness for old habits. That weakens them more than anything.

To stop obsessing over the mind's antics is not repression. It means remaining with love, with your innocence and goodness. You are placing your focus on something far more important. For example, let's imagine that a mother has lost her child in a crowd. She looks only for the face and listens only for the voice of her child. Because of her love she ignores everything except what is most important—finding her child. In the same way, we learn to stay focused on truth. This natural focus is how we confirm our true nature. It is not really a practice. A mother who searches for her lost child is not practicing to find her child. So do not think that your search for truth is a practice you perform. It is your life. It is a labor of love that delivers you into a life of grace.

11

Identity

Love is an aspect of our being. Like a diamond with many facets, love includes joy, honesty, and kindness. It is the awareness not merely of connection but of oneness. Love is the law of life. We can break this law through cruelty and other expressions of unconsciousness, but we cannot escape the profound moral consequences of doing so. It is impossible to act from separation without incurring a degree of suffering equal to the severity of the violation.

The full meaning of love is discovered through self-reflection. Only the moral sensitivity of our own conscience can empty us of what is less than love. Self-reflection is therefore the beginning of love, and self-knowledge its fulfilment. To understand ourselves is to love our own existence and then to find that existence equally in others.

We can say that in this love is the cure for all that ails us. Yet our access to the cure depends on insight. If I believe that I am a weak and selfish person by nature, then it will not make any sense to me when someone tells me to love myself unconditionally. How can I love such a flawed creature?

If I am not actually selfish but only fear that I am, then I only have to remove the belief. But if I am in fact quite selfish, and if I suffer other serious character problems related to self-ignorance, then it is certain that I suffer this ignorance and inflict it on others because I do not feel or know the reality of love.

In such a case, telling me to love myself will be relatively useless. It is precisely when we are in the grip of our delusion that we do not feel very loving. When our delusion is strong we do not know what love is or where to find it.

Without wisdom, our experience of love tends to be fleeting, sentimental, and tainted with sorrow. If you are already well established in wisdom, then you naturally love and you do not suffer. As long as you experience confusion and suffering, then inquiry is in order.

We can think of inquiry as the form love takes when it needs to clarify and deepen its roots in us. Unless the roots are strong, our attempts to grow up and outward to express the love that we are will be frustrated. The purpose of inquiry is not to fix or perfect the personality as if that would finally make us worthy of love. It is to liberate the personality from the burden of mistaken identity and thereby from the yardstick of perfection. There is no such thing as a perfect personality, but there is such thing as a personality that has become transparent to its source and is therefore at rest.

To rest deeply, you must first discover what makes you restless. This question turns your whole life into a search for truth. When you open yourself on that level a new power starts to move in your life. This power knows where to look and what to do with your life, and that is a great relief. The power of inquiry represents a degree of intelligence, or consciousness, that has been freed up from the automatism of habit and unconsciousness in us. It is now free to examine and observe, to convert more and more ignorance to intelligence.

Until we subject our lives to this examination it is as if we are stuck in a dark room that we have never explored. Our mind is like this room. It is the four-walled space of our apparent self. To begin with, we have to feel for where the walls are, how large is the room, whether there are windows we can open and whether the door is locked. For all we know the sun may be shining brilliantly outside. And it may be a grand and beautiful house we have inherited.

To explore the situation we can start to use our basic awareness and reason which, despite the darkness around us, are already fully present and functional. Inquiry means learning how to use awareness and intellect together to reveal truth. Within this darkened room, our first concern is to examine the darkness, not to blame the mind which is our tool.

When you are standing there in a pitch-black room, do you conclude that your eyes are a useless organ? No, you understand that the darkness is a temporary, external condition that can be replaced with light. Just as the eyes require light to see, the mind in its confused state requires a basic orientation, a mode of inquiry by which to illumine itself. When we are stuck in a limited sense of self, believing everything we think and feel, we have no recourse but to begin to observe and to reason our way out of this situation.

Can you consider that your own mind is the way? If it isn't, then where will you find it? Near death, the Buddha said, "Be a light unto yourselves." Jesus Christ said, "You are the light of the world." The light is your own heart and mind. To seek freedom somewhere outside of this ordinary, confused mind would be like looking for our keys on the sidewalk under a lamp post even though we lost them somewhere inside our darkened house. Either we illumine our mind or it remains in darkness. We cannot go somewhere else.

Illumined, mind becomes wisdom. When wisdom comes to the mind it comes as a whole, revealing wholeness, rejoicing in wholeness. This wholeness is also the nature of happiness, but our usual experience of happiness is hazy and all too brief because we have not understood its source. We experience happiness within a cloud of uncertainty as to how long it will last and how to make it stay.

Wholeness and happiness are usually veiled to us and seem to depend on special conditions to arise. This is a very frustrating mode of existence. Our completion then appears to exist in a thing, person, or life situation just beyond our present reach. Yet when we do manage to make the desired contact or achievement, we find that the thrill and bliss of it quickly fades and turns into something else. The objective, external triumph dissolves back into ordinary "me" with all the usual doubts and discontents.

The enjoyment derived from temporary experiences is more accurately called pleasure. Happiness is certainly a kind of pleasure, but pleasure alone does not encompass or establish happiness. Pleasure can be defined as a purely sensory level of happiness. If we are quite hungry and sit down to eat a meal in a beautiful restaurant with a pleasant companion, our pleasure will rise to a peak about midway through and then gradually return us back down to our normal condition.

If we are established in real happiness, the fading of that particular, momentary pleasure will leave us in a simple peace or contentment. If we are alienated from happiness, the end of that pleasure will bring a degree of anxiety or sorrow. This subtle suffering will drive us to grasp for the next pleasurable situation in an anxious attempt to regain a sense of hope and security.

The pleasure of other experiences, like falling in love, may last longer and include more nuances but they go the same way. There is no experience we can add to ourselves that does not, upon being assimilated, become normalized and absorbed into our default state of mind. Nor can we ever go outside of ourselves into an experience or environment to become something or someone else. All our travels are in imagination, and all imaginings end in disillusionment—literally the removal of illusions.

However, there is a way to approach experiences so that we take full pleasure in them while also opening the awareness of intrinsic happiness and wholeness. It is called the way of wisdom, or the process of enlightenment.

I would simply call it the spiritual life, but too often this is taken to mean a life of spiritualistic beliefs and morality without a radical shift of consciousness. For that reason I find it necessary and helpful to speak of enlightenment despite all the misunder-standings associated with the term.

The way of enlightenment is to dissolve the apparent, experiential divide between our habitual sense of self and that wondrous, expansive condition that we know as happiness, love, or oneness. It is entirely within our power to pass through the mysterious barricades of existential guilt, unworthiness, and fear—so that we can experience our lives as a constant unfolding of a subtler joy within. The subtlest pleasure of all is the sheer, awake clarity of presence.

So why do we remain dependent on the temporary happiness derived from limited pleasures and circumstances? Like someone who is addicted to a substance, our mind is clouded and we are not in a position to appreciate our options. To become ready to appreciate our options is the only purpose of suffering.

Suffering prods us out of passivity into active examination of our condition. We can call this a process of inquiry into self or reality. Self-inquiry means to observe and examine the whole of our experience in light of the questions: What is my nature? What is reality? What is truth?

Despite the various names we give to spiritual approaches and traditions, there is essentially no path other than this total, inner process of discovery. All apparent paths only reflect different facets and approaches to the same inner process.

Since our personal identity is where our mistaken view of reality roots itself, this is also where truth is revealed. By definition, truth is total and unchanging. It cannot be an opinion or point of view that contends with other views.

Truth, reality, and self must therefore be synonymous terms. You are the truth. You either know the truth in and through your own being or you despair that there is no truth in the world—because of course it is never found there, outside of ourselves.

To say that you are the light of the world means you are the reality of the world, the one who knows its existence. One's self, whatever that is, cannot possibility exist outside of reality or be other than what reality is. As truth is singular, discovering the truth must mean awakening in and as that reality rather than beholding it as an idea or image external to us.

Our identity is a function of understanding. In any given moment we are expressing the sum of who and what we understand ourselves to be. When our understanding changes then what we express and embody changes with it. If there is truth, then understanding is not just an intellectual game. It is a living force that cannot be separated from happiness. To understand is to be joyful, to be whole in your knowing, and therefore solid and spontaneous in action.

Identity is humanity's great riddle and taboo. To ask someone "Who are you?" is one of the most intimate, perplexing, and perhaps confrontational questions one could ask. Identity is the elephant in the room of human experience. Our lives are a flow of experiences, but where is the truth in all of it? Where do we find the bridge between the raw material of experiences on one side, and identity, truth, and meaning on the other?

The bridge is understanding the nature of experience. If the meaning of our experiences were something we could take at face value then we would never have any real question as to what is true. And therefore we would never suffer. Pleasure and pain would arrive and depart like weather patterns and there would be nothing to say about finding meaning or truth. But of course, there is plenty to say about these things, because the fact is that experience does not equal truth. Experience is not at all straightforward. Even as we claim the right to our own solipsistic version of truth called "my truth," we are constantly torn by competing ideas about what to make of our experiences. Eventually we have to face the fact that "our truth" is not the truth. It is simply our experience, which we may or may not have understood in terms of truth.

To understand experiences in terms of truth is called wisdom. Wisdom is the ability to perceive the universal within and behind the often confusing array of particulars. Traditionally, a wise person is one who can listen to any life situation and quickly provide a response that is both practical and profound. It is practical because it solves an immediate problem and it is profound because the solution simultaneously opens the person's consciousness to truth.

A wise person is one who helps us see through the fog of situations to the context that clarifies. To be able to do this, the wise must have removed their own attachment and identity from all mental, emotional, or worldly happenings. They do not effect this removal by asceticism but rather by insight. Insight removes illusion the same way light removes darkness—its nature just replaces it.

So what is the difference between experience and wisdom? In the relative world, we need sensory experience to know a thing. In the case of simple sensory phenomena, just seeing that thing—a cat, a cloud, an airplane—is enough to tell us what it basically is. That is relative knowledge born of sensory experience. This kind of knowledge expands immensely throughout our lives and yet it does not amount to wisdom.

It has been said that experience is the mother of wisdom. That is true, but wisdom also needs a father. We can experience the same painful patterns for days or decades without knowing how to end the cycle. To be caught in egoic consciousness means to be fooled by appearances, the surface qualities of our experiences.

Experience can be very misleading. For example, if I see a coiled rope at night I might believe it is a snake. The fear that I experience will be very real fear, but no amount of fear can make my mistaken perception true. Even if I have a very real heart attack due to fear, it was still a rope and not a snake.

Similarly, we might tell ourselves that depression is real, a disease even. Although the symptoms of depression are real experiences, these symptoms, like almost everything we think and feel, arise within a fictional, dream-like world of subjective perception.

Our entire identity or self-construct has arisen through this constant play of false associations and unquestioned assumptions. It consists of an intricate web of perceptual biases, cognitive distortions, secondhand knowledge, and reactive emotions that function automatically to create the gestalt experience of "myself."

The web was created through the process of pre-reflective identification from childhood onward. Pre-reflective identification means that without knowing what was happening, we linked our identity to our emotions and thoughts (or to others' emotions and thoughts). We drew conclusions about ourselves based on everyone and everything we encountered. It may be more accurate to say that the mind did this, since we were not exactly conscious of the process. The mind made its associations in conjunction with other more or less unconscious minds. In this way, we identified with our mental and emotional habits before we could possibly appreciate how relative and arbitrary these factors are.

Later in life, despite sensing the tenuous nature of our conditioned identity, we find ourselves clinging to that identity with a mixture of pride and shame. We want to accept ourselves and be accepted by others, yet we are not sure that this self is truly acceptable and worthy of love.

Which self is it, exactly, that we should accept? Moment after moment, in flashes of contentment or dissatisfaction, the mind presents us with a different image, idea, or feeling of who and how we are. Our sense of how life is going and what it all means is in constant flux.

If we knew our true nature, we would not be trying to figure out which idea of self to settle upon. We would exist in an atmosphere of lucid awareness and receptivity, free of clinging to any particular image. When we know the truth we have no need to believe anything in particular, whereas, for example, a person who harbors a lie has to work to remember and believe the lie.

If we find ourselves working hard to sustain a self-image, this means a false premise is at work. Through the dynamic of identification we are making an object of ourselves. When we objectify ourselves, we lack understanding and therefore compassion for our own experience. We will think, "I did that because I'm stupid," or, "I guess I'm just a selfish person." Such judgments preclude insight by imposing a moral assessment of our character.

Objectifying others in the same way, we will equally misunderstand them and fail to extend empathy. We will tend to see others as useful accessories to our happiness or as the resented cause of our unhappiness. This is the wounded, narcissistic core of egoic consciousness. This is hell.

When we imagine ourselves as just another object in the world, then meaning is exiled and projected away from the self. We can bear most any difficulty except the sense of meaninglessness and futility at the bottom of things. This primal sense of alienation has been called the knot in the heart. The knot is many things. It is a wound, a fortress, a repression barrier. It is the nihilistic belief that we are alone in a chaotic universe. It is a neglected and terrified child who defends himself with a force field of rage.

For some people rage is less prominent; apathy and numbness are stronger. In any case, it takes great courage and intelligence to face the knot of separation. Until we do so, we will dance like puppets on the strings of our unacknowledged suffering.

When we look with a clear and compassionate mind, we may find it incredible that we have all accepted so many unkind and downright crippling beliefs about ourselves. Yet there is a reason our mind-made identity is so convincing. It is the confluence of one absolutely real element, our conscious nature, and the hypnotizing play of mental phenomena within it. The real element lends its reality to the illusion, at least until we get wise to the game.

It is like starting with a blank piece of paper and then having a master artist draw a seemingly three-dimensional object on it. Like the paper, our consciousness provides the background potential on which the illusion can be created and then believed.

To dehypnotize ourselves we must make the distinction between the background, observing awareness and the foreground activity and contents of mind. In other words, we have to look at the aspect of our experience that is not moving, which is awareness.

Initially, one might wonder what this awareness has to do with truth, since it is a neutral, silent presence. Awareness never asserts anything. But insofar as we recognize that awareness remains unchanged by our experiences, we break up the hypnosis of identifying with moods and mind states.

This insight allows us to see our experiences for what they are, without projection, fear, and grasping. As we stop identifying with our states of mind we will cease to objectify ourselves and others. The object view of self will collapse and no longer make any sense to us.

Identification is a habit of contracting awareness around mind states, lending apparent solidity to what is insubstantial. Thus for all its apparent solidity, our egoic contraction is simply a great, heavy cloud that has taken shape in our consciousness. To see clouds for clouds and sun for sun is enlightenment. The sun (consciousness) can shine through the clouds because it is an essentially stable factor, while they are not.

Just as a cloud is not a solid and stable fixture in the sky, we do not possess something solid inside us called an ego. Ego is not a real part of us like a limb or an organ. It is not our personality, our body, our inner child, or our feelings. Ego is just our confused relationship to all these things. It is a mode of perception, a belief system. When we truly see through it, it disappears.

Ego literally means "self." For better or worse, this is the name that we give to our delusion, since that delusion takes up residence in our sense of self. Once we dispel the delusion, our personality and desires will function much differently. We will experience the real nature of self in a radically uplifted and expanded context.

12

Meditation

The most well-known method for illumining the mind is meditation. Though it often takes the form of sitting down in silence for a period of time, meditation means more than this. The spiritual life is in large part a process of observing, and meditation is a focused, formalized practice of observing. As such it is a microcosm of the search for truth.

When we live a meditative life we are living in the atmosphere of our true nature, so as to fully recognize and actualize its qualities. Meditation is the atmosphere of looking and listening. At first this atmosphere is mainly filled with doubts, questions, and restlessness, which is natural. Restlessness means that because our identification with thought is very strong, our attention leaps from thought to thought without knowing where to rest.

The solution is not to stop thinking but rather to dissolve our identification with thought. Our identification with thoughts is the fuel for their proliferation. No matter how difficult it feels to observe thoughts without getting lost in them, the fact is that observing gradually works to break the bond.

Therefore the first aim of meditation is to develop stability and clarity of attention. To that end, a focused concentration on the breath can be used until a more open mode of attention is possible. As stability deepens, one can use the breath as a gentle anchor within the broader awareness of the field of the body.

Eventually, attention during meditation can become so lucid, expansive, and stable that it is no longer a focused state of attention—it is just awareness in its natural condition. At that point there is no sense of effort involved in holding attention, and there is no special idea of meditating or not meditating. There is only awareness being aware, as it always is.

At this level we feel and know that meditation is our nature. After the initial phase of actively training our attention, the recognition of natural stability takes over. From here our insight and clarity grows exponentially, and with the guidance of a qualified teacher, realization becomes inevitable.

Whereas we once saw periods of meditation as carefully carved-out breaks from being lost in the maelstrom of our activities, we now experience meditation as a natural mode of being that subsumes every moment of thought, speech, and action in daily life. We no longer see sitting meditation as an exotic or daunting practice but rather as a welcome time to dive deeper into the clear light of our being.

Thus the primary goal of meditation is insight, not stillness. Stillness is only a relative aid and a wonderful byproduct of meditation. This understanding frees us from the myth that enlightenment is a blank, thoughtless state of mind that we enter through meditation.

When seekers say, "I try to meditate, but my mind never stops," it is a clear indication that the myth of enlightenment as a state of "no thought" is at work. The absence of thoughts is not liberation—not only because thoughts inevitably return but more importantly because thoughts are not the problem. Even if one could make thoughts stop permanently it would not amount to self-realization.

A closely related myth is that if our true nature consists of direct wisdom unmediated by concepts, then we can reach this wisdom by preemptively rejecting all concepts and forms of knowledge as useless and empty.

This myth encourages people to dismiss common sense and reasoning as though they are obstacles to awakening. It suggests that if we avoid critical thinking of any kind—confusing it with judgmentalism—and simply proclaim that we "don't know anything," then we are living the radical truth.

It should be clear that rejecting concepts is not the same as realizing the truth beyond concepts. Rejection only fixates us further in ignorance, because it means we have assumed that the apparent world, and the conceptual intellect that makes sense of it, is somehow separate from the spirit. Although it is true that conceptual knowledge is limited and does not capture the absolute nature of reality, it is entirely valid and useful within its own sphere.

The mistake is when all we know is relative concepts and we seek absolute truth there. Being identified with the conceptual mind creates great constriction and despair. Eventually, we realize that worldly knowledge cannot reveal meaning and essence. This problem is solved not by rejecting knowledge but by realizing the absolute.

From the absolute point of view, which is our very being, we have no need to reject anything. We see the relative as pervaded and contained by the absolute.

In other words, no matter how complex and varied the universe or mind appears to be, this complexity of finite perception and thought exists within the infinite, absolute order of consciousness, the quintessence of simplicity. The simplicity of formless, aware intelligence does not vitiate complexity of form. It only affirms, as Winston Churchill said, that intense complexities give rise to intense simplicities.

A mind that rejects conceptual knowledge falls prey to relativism, a denial of all normative standards of knowledge and ethics. People have always sought freedom by dispensing with social norms and boundaries. One who is liberated from the human dream may feel free to break a taboo at times, but the mere breaking of taboos does not make you free.

You can spend your whole life pushing boundaries or having no boundaries, and surely making a big mess of your life, but you would still be stuck firmly within the boundaries of experience.

You would still be looking for freedom in a state of mind or circumstance.

Some voices urge us to find freedom by giving full rein to our instinctive impulses and desires. This is sometimes dressed up in spiritual language as following where the energy or "shakti" wants to go. Although lifting the unnecessary suppression and shame we may have accumulated is a positive step, we have to see that fulfilling our every whim and desire will not make us any freer than stifling them.

People who follow raw desire and energy tend to get stuck in a self-absorbed, rather adolescent cycle of excitement and depression as they constantly ask themselves what great, subterranean desire or intuition they should be following to the other side of the earth in search of full vitality. This temptation is especially strong when we have opened the storehouse of bliss and ordinary experiences become far more pleasurable. Ultimately, the powerful energy of bliss must be penetrated by insight and embraced by the greater joy of peace. When we are well situated in our real nature we do not feel squeezed by the ordinary limitations of life.

The next common myth about enlightenment, and the goal of meditation, is that it is a state of oneness reached by merging with the physical world or otherwise altering our experience of awareness. Various esoteric teachings and practices, perhaps taken out of context, have contributed to this idea. Yet we do not have to expand awareness outside of the body, locate it behind or above the head, bring it up through the chakras, or bring it down from the heavens into the heart. It is neither necessary nor possible to manipulate the basic nature of awareness.

The attempt to reach a spatial, physical oneness with the world is an expression of materialism, the belief that we are essentially a body. If we identify as a physical object we will seek oneness by joining with other objects. In awareness there is no separative mind that needs to merge into space or to feel especially delighted with every little thing in the world. Awareness itself is the delight and connection, which the world highlights and reflects back to us.

The meaning of oneness is not found out there in space. All space, and everything perceived in space, exists only within our awareness. There is no possibility of expanding what is already infinite and indivisible. All the physical space in the universe amounts to nothing as compared with the nonspatial, boundless intelligence of consciousness in which all space appears.

Though we do experience the world through the localized position of the body, and our sensory data are therefore limited, these sense limitations do not indicate the limits of consciousness. In the presence of light, the eyes allow us to see a certain distance, yet this tells us nothing about where the light ends or where it comes from. When we say that consciousness is infinite, this cannot be validated or invalidated by sensory data.

We do not need to see, hear, or feel in an unusual way to know undivided awareness as reality. We can know it directly through realization. Once we know essence, we do not need to go further out into appearance.

When the core sense of separation is dissolved, we feel ourselves transparent and intimate with life. We feel no need to go anywhere or to obtain extraordinary, psychic knowledge of past, future, or otherwise distant things to know this oneness. We will not be seeking oneness in heightened sensory experiences, intense feelings, or a dissociated state of awareness. We will feel and know the oneness of existence through direct identity with all beings, which is love.

What all of this means with regard to meditation is that it should be understood as the clarification of awareness rather than the arresting or altering of mind states. In meditation we learn to observe everything as it is, from our inner feeling states to the stones and trees around us. By intently witnessing there arises the awareness that all perceptions and cognitions are passing through us. We thereby sense the oneness of the observer and the observed, while learning that the observer is never changed by what it beholds.

When I speak of the observer I am not referring to a personal self. It is always awareness that observes. There is no lower, personal observer that is transcended by a higher, impersonal observer. Though one thinks, "It is my mind that observes," or, "I am observing," all observing occurs within and through the naked, mirrorlike presence of awareness.

As we settle deeper in observing, we gain an ever sharper insight to our momentary habits, motivations, and the emotional-energetic states they create. This keen insight liberates us from the movement of escape and distortion.

For example, most people experience some fear of solitude, silence, and inactivity. When we inhabit these moments with presence, we eventually penetrate the surface of restless insecurity and open in spacious well-being, without need for any content or movement to distract us. As we learn to live in this receptivity, we can feel the movement of life arising as a bridge from the emptiness of pure consciousness to the somethingness of endeavors and relationships.

In this clarified receptivity, when we are neither trying to escape nor force the movement of life. We have the feeling that action is happening on its own, moving through us rather than managed by a superfluous thinking process. This is the experience of spontaneous action that all sages describe.

To understand the meaning of spontaneity, we can compare the separative mode of experience versus the undivided mode. In the first mode we suffer chronic doubt about our choices because we are not sure what principles to act upon. As our actions are often unwise and produce negative results, we have every reason to question what we are doing. We cannot help but to question, for we have not understood the basis for right action.

The experience of spontaneous action is simply the consequence of a clear mind. Just as riding a bicycle feels effortless once we have learned how, wisdom once established sets our actions on the right basis, allowing us to act without confusion. This does not mean that we will never think or plan. One might do some intentional, constructive thinking about a course of action, but this kind of thought is much different from the chaotic chatter of a mind that has not found clarity. Likewise, engaging in a reasonable degree of planning for an endeavor is entirely different from neurotically planning out one's life to ensure future happiness.

When the mind has been clarified by insight, we do continue to think, feel, and reason, but we experience these processes as part of the flow of life. Prior to insight, we experienced those faculties as if behind a veil that separates us from life. On one side of the veil was "my mind," and on the other side was life. The seeming veil or division between self and life gives us the sense of being a separate thinker, agent, or doer who must navigate an alien world.

When we dissolve the veil, then our thinking, feeling, and doing is felt to arise within life itself, within the intelligent space of awareness. Sages experience thought as transparent and empty. Thought moves freely according to the object being considered.

By understanding the nature of experience, we establish the basis for appropriate action, which is the meaning of morality. Morality does not come from abstract idealism but rather from natural laws of cause and effect. Real morality is established through our awakened intelligence and sensitivity, never as a conceptual ideal or dogma.

The simple meaning of morality is that we act from love and wisdom. When we have seen through immature approaches to happiness, we conduct our relationships and endeavors with the awareness of appropriate ethics.

Through the stillness of meditation we clarify action, and through its solitude we reach the basis for togetherness. Eventually we meditate in total ease, without seeking or wanting anything from the mind and emotions. This ease exists prior to meditation and continues afterward, as activities resume. The innocence of awareness surpasses cleverness. Its simplicity surpasses complexity.

13

Self-Love

What we call the heart is a reliable touchstone of our spiritual maturity. We do not have to think of the heart as separate from the mind. The heart is a metaphor for feeling, sensitivity, and attitude, all of which are deeply connected with how we think.

In this existence, we know that love exists but it seems to be scarce or elusive. It seems to be outside of us. And so the question is how do we access love? How do we experience or receive love, especially if we have never had the early childhood experience of feeling deeply loved? We cannot tell a person in this condition just to accept that they are love. That will not work. There is a process of discovery that must happen.

In a sense, love can indeed be found outside of us—it can be communicated to us by those who have a knowledge of love. When we receive the communication of love from our parents as children, or from someone else who is able and understands how to love, then it seems that we have discovered a stream of life-giving water and we are dependent on that stream. We are going to do everything we can to sustain that experience, to continue drinking from that stream.

The trouble is that everyone comes to a point of seeing that no matter how much love one gets from outside, whether from a friend or spouse or healer, it is not enough. It is not going to be enough because it is still perceived as outside of you.

Once you have gotten in touch with the feeling of shared understanding and togetherness, you reach a point where you say, "I'm a bit dependent on this source, and I'm still not entirely healed. I'm clinging to this source, person, or relationship. What do I have to do to bridge this gap so that the love is within me?"

The first step is to acknowledge what love you do feel,

because what you acknowledge grows. You love something in this world—someone, some place, some form of beauty, some activity. There is a goodness and richness that you feel in relation to something. And as you acknowledge that your sense of love and beauty is evoked by these things, you can start to trace its source, asking, "What is it that I love?"

What you love is the well-being and wholeness that you feel when you are in contact with that object or experience. With that insight you begin to dissolve the sense of separation—the idea that the love is coming from the object and not from you. For example, when you hear music that evokes love, the music has reminded you of what is within you. The beauty and devotion that the song evokes belongs to your own nature, not to the song itself.

You realize that this quality is within you, though you are not usually cognizant of it. For some time, you have to seek that evocation. You have to evoke that remembrance by creating an atmosphere of beauty around you. Sanctify the space and actions of your daily life. Go to places where you more easily feel that sacredness.

There then comes a time when you break through the sense of division, when you feel that you no longer need the middleman of that place or activity to evoke the fullness of love. You cease to rely on that externality. And you will eventually find that you no longer fall in love in the same way. It is impossible. You rise in love. The love is not really coming from the other. It just is. Then the relationship is just a reflection of the love you already feel within. Love has become a simple reality for you. It is your very self and yet that self is universal.

There is a poem by Pablo Neruda that hints at that state of being. He writes,

I love you without knowing how, or when or from where.
I love you straightforwardly, without complexities or pride;

So I love you because I know no other way.

When you are in the immediacy of this love you simply love others, regardless of whether they are a romantic partner or not. There is a connection that resonates, especially if the other is in the same awareness.

If that is not yet your experience, then I would encourage you to keep acknowledging what love you do feel. Seek to extend and express it, because this is what heals the mind. What heals is not just to receive love—that's just a beginning—but to see that you have love to give. If you are depressed and someone comes to your door starving or injured, you would help that person. And by giving to that person you would be uplifted and taken out of your depression. Depression is a closing in upon oneself in isolation, whereas when the heart is outgoing with its love, one cannot be depressed. Only in the giving of love do we find purpose, connection, and sanity. There is no cure for depression within the energetic field of depression. A new energy has to enter the equation, which is the energy of communication and giving.

So at some point the only healing for you is to simply be love and to look to give constantly. By acknowledging your love you cease to wait for the reflection of love from outside of you. It is always here now.

Continue acknowledging love and you will approach the removal of that duality, which is the greatest healing that a human being can experience. This brings us back to the innocence we once knew but were not fully conscious of and able to carry forward as we grew up.

In a poem called "Love After Love," Derek Walcott speaks about this great homecoming:

The time will come
when, with elation

you will greet yourself arriving
at your own door, in your own mirror
and each will smile at the other's welcome,

and say, sit here. Eat.
You will love again the stranger who was your self.
Give wine. Give bread. Give back your heart
to itself, to the stranger who has loved you

all your life, whom you ignored
for another, who knows you by heart.
Take down the love letters from the bookshelf,

the photographs, the desperate notes,
peel your own image from the mirror.
Sit. Feast on your life.

The reason you have to peel your image from the mirror is that an image of yourself can never measure up to what you are. Initially we used the image to create a sense of security. Gradually our self-image revealed its inadequacy to house our spirit, its majesty and its freedom. The image turned into a set of self-judgments, hopes, and fears. In one moment it smiled and promised you would someday be enough. In the next moment it spoke with a voice of self-loathing and shame.

You had written love letters, the poet says, kept photographs, wrote in journals about your thoughts and feelings. But your distance from yourself—your underlying rejection and neglect of your real being—kept your attention focused on fleeting and fragmentary reflections of love.

The mind is the mirror. We placed images on the mirror; we placed our dreams there and we told ourselves many stories when we felt lonely and wanted to hear a voice, any voice. The mirror itself is not the problem. The mind was only doing its job of reflection. Like a computer, it gave you back whatever you put into it.

When we peel the image from the mirror, we find the mirror is perfectly clean and bright. The mind like a diamond reflects the light of consciousness, love, and creativity. When our search for love finally leads us to peel off the images and gaze in that mirror long enough, what we behold is the intrinsic benevolence of spirit.

Perhaps we turn away and entertain images again, only to take them down again and gaze some more, acquainting with the pure love and wholeness arising in consciousness. Gradually we gain confidence that the mirror of the mind is always going to reflect the original, unchanging truth of our being, and that we simply have to get used to this new view.

The view from love's eyes is often more perfect than we can stand. It seems unbelievable that we can make this shift and stop squeezing ourselves back into a small and disempowered view. It feels like such a bold and daring step because love, we realize, is not weak. Love is very strong. A person who knows their nature as love is gentle and kind but is also incredibly strong and cannot be manipulated.

When deep love shines within, as your nature and as the vision through which you see others, then you can look at the ugliest, most painful aspects of life and not recoil. This love will root itself in the ground of practical insight and action. For love is true power and communication. When you come home to love you no longer desire substitute powers. You see that all other powers rely on a break in communication, a form of dishonesty or separation. From the standpoint of our true nature, power is a meaningless idea because power is what we use to get something. The real power is to share in what is real.

14

Listening

If I had not met my death in silence
I would still be dead with noise.
Now I am like a hidden spring
around which the deep and green life
grows.

In the effort to love ourselves unconditionally, we find that love does not pertain to an objectified self. As soon as I try to turn love upon myself as an object, I cannot exactly find myself. But the intention to love myself has an intelligence within it. It evokes a softening of self-objectification or judgment, such that a new sense of space, openness, and mercy arises. I do not even know who is the self I can love. I just see an innocent body and mind in front of me, a mind that is trying to find the way.

In seeking to love myself, I dissolve my self-fixation and the feeling of love becomes universal, because that is how love really is. Thus I realize I am not a lovable or unlovable object. This pure beingness is what I am, and love is.

We tend to fear love because it feels like a kind of death. The fear of death is the anchor of all our fear. We are afraid of death because we are not intimate enough with what death means for us, which is that we cannot hold onto the physical or any situation in the physical. If we would really face this we would see that the only real power we have is to love.

If we give our attention totally to that we undergo ego death. In that death we could say fear dies, and when it dies we see that fear had taken the shape of my self. When the shape collapses, a great energy of presence is released and this is where attention is now rooted. It then becomes difficult to consider the future much. Attention is rooted in the present moment and energy flows from consciousness into the purposes of the moment.

From this understanding we can see that we do not need to get into the present moment. We are already there. What we need is to clarify our relationship to this moment. The clarity is to know that you do not have to suffer the hypnosis of all the thoughts and feelings that pass through. Some of them are constructive and beautiful and some are not. As you watch, you learn to recognize what is coming from intelligence and what is coming from confusion.

This moment always brings a new experience, a new situation. As we recognize our freedom, we begin to wield a new power to dispense with what is negative in our lives. We will easily shed bad habits or unhealthy relationships. We will know when our feelings are alerting us to something important to speak about or act upon, or when our feelings are coming from our own projections. This is discovered through listening.

A human being who listens grows very quickly. A human being who does not know how to listen to self or to others will suffer greatly. Listen to this moment, to all that is happening within you and around you. To listen is to create space for love to enter. To listen is to be heard by life.

Listening is deeply connected with the quality of humility. The humble can hear. When you have humility you have the key to everything else. Humility is to be ready to say I don't know, I'm sorry, or I forgive, without feeling that you are losing something. You are only losing your pride and gaining the world. When you have pride you will feel, either now or later, terribly cut off from others, alienated and unloved. When you sacrifice pride your sense of belonging and connection is restored.

Humility is another word for being transparent. To have the light of being shine through, we have to stop taking our self to be an object. The source of obstruction is always objectification, a fixed judgment or view.

The right attitude toward the mind and toward everything else in creation is forgiveness and appreciation. Keep coming back to the simplicity of being. You are the knowing, the knower. With this understanding you will bring a lot of light to others. The impact of your illumination spreads out infinitely and there is no way to measure it.

Eventually, all exotic notions about spirituality disappear. Life is spiritual. You have been transformed by insight or you have not. You work with difficulties through love and humor, or you do not. You are honest with yourself about mistakes made, or you are not.

There is no way to measure how deeply enlightened you are. You alone know to what extent you are happy and free in all aspects of your life. And if someone asks you whether you are enlightened, why not just admit to knowing you are the light of consciousness, like everything and everyone else.

BOOKS

O-BOOKS

SPIRITUALITY

O is a symbol of the world, of oneness and unity; this eye represents knowledge and insight. We publish titles on general spirituality and living a spiritual life. We aim to inform and help you on your own journey in this life.

If you have enjoyed this book, why not tell other readers by posting a review on your preferred book site? Recent bestsellers from O-Books are:

Heart of Tantric Sex
Diana Richardson
Revealing Eastern secrets of deep love and intimacy to Western couples.
Paperback: 978-1-90381-637-0 ebook: 978-1-84694-637-0

Crystal Prescriptions
The A-Z guide to over 1,200 symptoms and their healing crystals
Judy Hall
The first in the popular series of five books, this handy little guide is packed as tight as a pill-bottle with crystal remedies for ailments.
Paperback: 978-1-90504-740-6 ebook: 978-1-84694-629-5

Take Me To Truth
Undoing the Ego
Nouk Sanchez, Tomas Vieira
The best-selling step-by-step book on shedding the Ego, using
the teachings of *A Course In Miracles*.
Paperback: 978-1-84694-050-7 ebook: 978-1-84694-654-7

The 7 Myths about Love...Actually!
The journey from your HEAD to the HEART of your SOUL
Mike George
Smashes all the myths about LOVE.
Paperback: 978-1-84694-288-4 ebook: 978-1-84694-682-0

The Holy Spirit's Interpretation of the New Testament
A course in Understanding and Acceptance
Regina Dawn Akers
Following on from the strength of *A Course In Miracles*, NTI
teaches us how to experience the love and oneness of God.
Paperback: 978-1-84694-085-9 ebook: 978-1-78099-083-5

The Message of A Course In Miracles
A translation of the text in plain language
Elizabeth A. Cronkhite
A translation of *A Course in Miracles* into plain, everyday
language for anyone seeking inner peace. The companion
volume, *Practicing A Course In Miracles*, offers practical lessons
and mentoring.
Paperback: 978-1-84694-319-5 ebook: 978-1-84694-642-4

Rising in Love
My Wild and Crazy Ride to Here and Now, with Amma, the
Hugging Saint
Ram Das Batchelder
Rising in Love conveys an author's extraordinary journey of

spiritual awakening with the Guru, Amma.
Paperback: 978-1-78279-687-9 ebook: 978-1-78279-686-2

Thinker's Guide to God
Peter Vardy
An introduction to key issues in the philosophy of religion.
Paperback: 978-1-90381-622-6

Your Simple Path
Find happiness in every step
Ian Tucker
A guide to helping us reconnect with what is really important in our lives.
Paperback: 978-1-78279-349-6 ebook: 978-1-78279-348-9

Body of Wisdom
Women's Spiritual Power and How it Serves
Hilary Hart
Bringing together the dreams and experiences of women across the world with today's most visionary spiritual teachers.
Paperback: 978-1-78099-696-7 ebook: 978-1-78099-695-0

Dying to Be Free
From Enforced Secrecy to Near Death to True Transformation
Hannah Robinson
After an unexpected accident and near-death experience, Hannah Robinson found herself radically transforming her life, while a remarkable new insight altered her relationship with her father; a practising Catholic priest.
Paperback: 978-1-78535-254-6 ebook: 978-1-78535-255-3